# Pet Pages unleashed!

## Fetching Ideas For Animal-Inspired Scrapbook Pages

From The Editors of Memory Makers Books

MEMORY MAKERS BOOKS

Denver, Colorado

W9-CCQ-230

*MANAGING EDITOR* MaryJo Regier
*EDITOR* Emily Curry Hitchingham
*ART DIRECTOR* Nick Nyffeler
*GRAPHIC DESIGNERS* Jordan Kinney, Robin Rozum
*ART ACQUISITIONS EDITOR* Janetta Abucejo Wieneke
*CRAFT EDITOR* Jodi Amidei
*PHOTOGRAPHER* Ken Trujillo
*CONTRIBUTING PHOTOGRAPHER* Jennifer Reeves
*PHOTO STYLIST* Kevin Hardiek
*CONTRIBUTING WRITER* Heather A. Eades
*ASSISTANT ART ACQUISITIONS EDITOR* Karen Cain
*EDITORIAL SUPPORT* Amy Glander, Cindy Kacynski, Kelli Noto, Lydia Rueger, Dena Twinem, Anne Wilbur
*CONTRIBUTING MEMORY MAKERS MASTERS* Jenn Brookover, Torrey Scott, Shannon Taylor, Angelia Wigginton

Memory Makers® *Pet Pages Unleashed*

Copyright © 2006 Memory Makers Books
All rights reserved.

The ideas in this book are for the personal use of the scrapbooker. By permission of the publisher, they may
be either hand-traced or photocopied to make single copies, but under no circumstances may they be resold or
republished. No other part of this book may be reproduced in any form, or by any electronic or mechanical means,
including information storage and retrieval systems, without permission in writing from the publisher,
except by a reviewer, who may quote brief passages in a review.

Published by Memory Makers Books, an imprint of F+W Publications, Inc.
12365 Huron Street, Suite 500, Denver, CO  80234
Phone (800) 254-9124

First edition. Printed in the United States.

10 09 08 07 06 5 4 3 2 1

Library of Congress Cataloging-in-Publication Data

Pet pages unleashed : fetching ideas for animal-inspired scrapbook pages / [Emily Curry
    Hitchingham, editor].-- 1st ed.
        p. cm.
    Includes bibliographical references and index.
    ISBN-13: 978-1-892127-72-3
    ISBN-10: 1-892127-72-5
    1. Photographs--Conservation and restoration. 2. Photograph albums. 3. Scrapbooks. 4.
Pets.  I. Hitchingham, Emily Curry.

TR465.P46 2006
745.593--dc22

                                                                2005056265

Distributed to trade and art markets by

F+W Publications, Inc.
4700 East Galbraith Road,
Cincinnati, OH 45236
Phone (800) 289-0963

Distributed in Canada by
Fraser Direct
100 Armstrong Avenue
Georgetown, ON, Canada  L7G 5S4
Tel: (905) 877-4411

Distributed in the U.K. and Europe by
David & Charles
Brunel House, Newton Abbot, Devon,
TQ12 4PU, England
Tel: (+44) 1626 323200, Fax: (+44) 1626 323319
E-mail: mail@davidandcharles.co.uk

Distributed in Australia by
Capricorn Link
P.O. Box 704, S. Windsor NSW,
2756 Australia
Tel: (02) 4577-3555

Memory Makers Books is the home of *Memory Makers*, the scrapbook magazine dedicated to educating and
inspiring scrapbookers. To subscribe, or for more information, call (800) 366-6465.
Visit us on the Internet at www.memorymakersmagazine.com.

*Dedicated to* pet-loving scrapbookers and the cherished animal companions that inspired the pages inside. May you continue to create wonderful warm and fuzzy memories in the pleasure of each other's company.

# Table Of Contents

## chapter **one**

## chapter **two**

## chapter **three**

### Pet Personalities 64-91

Pages that portray the unique
characteristics and qualities of pets

## chapter **four**

### Pets and Their Favorite People 92-119

Pages that pay tribute to the
bond between pets and the
people who love them

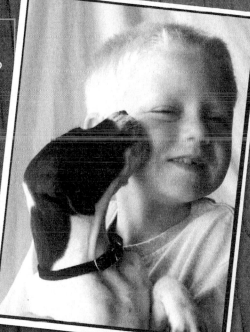

**Bonus creature feature fun facts**

# "...Fletch, our... much-beloved 'first baby.'"

best friend

fletch • paws • play
wet nose • dog bones
• going for walks • cute dog

**fletch**

How is it we got so lucky? Out of all of the puppies in the world, we managed to somehow find the very best one. From the day we brought Fletch home, he has been the most loving, loyal, tender-hearted companion. Always eager to play, always eager to be "lovey." We simply could not have asked for a better pet and furry family member. And no matter how many children we someday have, in our hearts, Fletch will always be our "first baby."
Nov. 2005

• fun friend

What would we be without our pets? In their selfless, silent way, animals introduce a companionship into our lives without want of anything in return but our attention and affection—perhaps the most simple but treasured of friendships. And for the joy and devotion they faithfully bestow, we should all aspire to deserve the high esteem with which our pets seem to hold us.

If you're like me, home has always been a place that included pets. While growing up, I was never without a menagerie of animals—hamsters, rabbits, fish, birds—then there were Muffin and Izzi, the family dogs. Following college, I was finally able to fill the void in my heart that the restrictions of dorms and rental apartments had for years left empty—I could adopt and once again share my home with a special pet. By sheer fortune my now-husband and I came upon Fletch, our sweet cocker spaniel and much-beloved "first baby." Seven years and countless memories later, it is hard to remember the time before Fletch joined our family. As animal lovers, I'm sure you'll agree, pets are indeed family members. They add warmth to the household and inspire laughter and lightheartedness in ways that didn't exist before they came along—and we find ourselves all the better for having our cherished pets in our lives.

With that said, our scrapbooks are as much a place for our pets as their rightful place in our families. In addition to preserving precious pet memories, these pages represent the story of our pets' lives—stories only we can document. And besides, let's not forget how FUN it is to create pet pages! As you'll be endearingly reminded of in the artwork to come, animals are sources of sheer joy, never short on humor, irresistibly ornery and abounding with the most touching and tender of spirits. And as if charming page examples aren't enough get you inspired, we've also included numerous helpful bonus features such as checklists and idea prompts, pet album examples, pet facts, quotes and so much more.

So get ready to spend some quality time with your favorite furry, feathered, finned or amphibious family member. After all, remember, it's attention and affection they want most from you. Well, that and maybe a treat or two.

Enjoy!

*Emily*

Emily Curry Hitchingham, Associate Editor

# chapter one | Welcome Home

The moment your eyes connect with those of an animal meant just for you, an inexplicable bond between two hearts is forever forged, and you simply know...this one is The One. The adoption of a pet is a blessing of learning as much as you teach, receiving as much as you give, and discovering that some of the biggest of hearts reside in the smallest of bodies. Scrapbook the amazing love story shared with your newest family member right from the beginning so that you may look back weeks, months, even years from now to see how you both have grown.

# Girl

# Pretty

*I can't say enough about Tessie, she is such an amazing dog!*
*Our family is so in love with her. She has been such a loyal faithful*
*Companion, not just for my husband and I but for our 2 children.*
*She has put up with countless ear pulling, tackles and hair pulling*
*From little ones, and never once even moved. I love that she is protective*
*Of our house and our family, and that she does not like any man but my*
*Husband. I can not believe we were lucky enough to go to the Humane*
*Society and happen to find her that day, it was fate that we were to have*
*This wonderful dog, and one fact that is crystal clear, she is a very Pretty*
*Girl and we love her with all our hearts! Tessie 2004*

## Pretty Girl

From their first encounter at the Humane Society, Tessie and her soon-to-be family were destined to be together. Becky's layout was inspired by Tessie's black and white spots, which are reflected in her use of circles and polka-dot prints. The family calls Tessie by her nickname, "Pretty Girl," so Becky used frills, flowers and pink accents to celebrate this much-beloved princess in chic feminine style.

Becky Heisler, Waupaca, Wisconsin

**Supplies:** Patterned paper (DieCuts with a View, Doodlebug Design, Imagination Project); textured cardstock (Bazzill); paper flowers (Prima); ribbon (Offray); embroidery floss; transparency; stamping ink

**Puppies** under 6 months of age require an average of **five hours** of care per day (in 20-minute increments) to raise, train and socialize properly.

## 4 Boys & a Girl

Slightly overwhelmed by all the "love" Jenn's four boys were so eager to pour upon her after she was brought home, sweet little Katy sat quietly nonetheless for this adorable photo. Jenn incorporated the same aesthetics into this computer-generated layout as are found in traditional paper designs by layering digital paper, overlays and text for a sense of depth. She highlighted the number "4" and set it inside a patterned circle. By placing the overlay at the end and reducing its opacity, Jenn accomplished the realistic look of a traditional page.

**Jenn Brookover, San Antonio, Texas**

**Supplies:** Patterned paper, sanded overlay (Shabby Mommy Kit, www.shabbyprincess.com); circle brush (Rhonna Farrer's Peace Out Kit, www.twopeasinabucket.com); ribbon (source unknown)

## Killian

Carmel's computer-generated layout bubbles over with joyful effervescence in celebration of sweet Killian's adoption. The festive and fun look of the digital papers creates the illusion of bubbles being blown in excitement, with a metal-rimmed tag element slightly overlapping the birds-eye view photo. The vibrant look of Killian's page was all part of a digital kit, which Carmel manipulated into this Welcome Home party on "paper."

**Carmel Flores, Westfield, Indiana**

**Supplies:** Scrapbooking elements (Sweet Sprinkles Kit, www.shabbyprincess.com)

Our House Has Grown
by 4 ~~Feet~~ paws

*After the wedding and right before Wendy and Kevin left for their few days at the cabin on Monday, they went to pick up their new puppy. Wendy had decided that her next puppy would be named Fernie – yes after the ski hill! They got him from dads boss, Brian at the farm. He is a black lab mixed with something unknown.*

*He was very quiet and peaceful that day they brought him to visit us. A few hours later, once he settled, he did find his voice! He loves to bark so that everyone knows where he is! Fernie travels well – which is good as they take a lot of weekend trips to Swift Current to visit family and friends.*

Fernie

## Our House Has Grown by 4 Paws

Two days after Melanie's sister and brother-in-law were married, they added a new addition to their family—Fernie. Melanie created this two-page spread to document Fernie's arrival home and as a means of looking back to see how much he's grown! Warm, textural-looking papers set a loving tone for the layout, and torn edges evoke a look of playful puppy nibbles.

Melanie Gatzke, Lethbridge, Alberta, Canada

**Supplies:** Patterned paper (Daisy D's); rub-on letters, staples (Making Memories, Provo Craft); heart brads (Provo Craft); heart buttons (Jesse James); cardstock; chalk ink

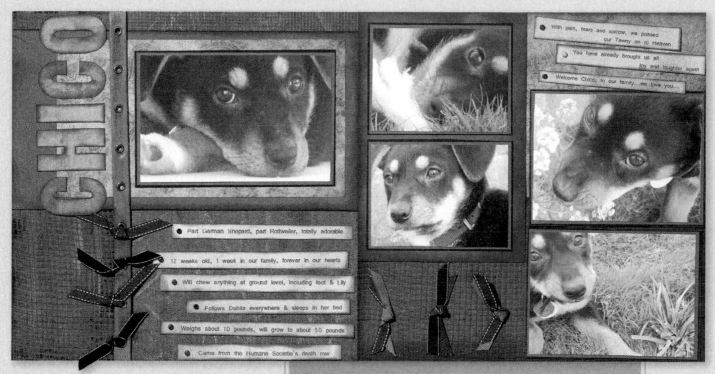

Scrapbook page for Chico, featuring photos and journaling strips:
- CHICO (title)
- With pain, tears and sorrow, we passed our Tawny on to Heaven
- You have already brought us all joy and laughter again
- Welcome Chico, to our family...we love you...
- Part German Sheperd, part Rottweiler, totally adorable
- 12 weeks old, 1 week in our family, forever in our hearts
- Will chew anything at ground level, including feet & Lily
- Follows Dahlia everywhere & sleeps in her bed
- Weighs about 10 pounds, will grow to about 50 pounds
- Came from the Humane Societie's death row

# Chico

Following the loss of their much-beloved previous dog, the Zouari family rescued Chico from the Humane Society—and, it turns out, he rescued them right back. Deanna created this page as a warm extension of welcoming this precious puppy into their hearts, using rich textures of handmade quilted paper, leather and mesh, as well as the colors found in Chico's coat. She embellished each page with ribbons, tying them through a leather eyelet trim on the left page and adhering them directly onto the right page. Journaling strips on both pages share sweet sentiments and puppy facts, accented with coordinating brads.

**Deanna Zouari, Avondale, Arizona**

**Supplies:** Patterned papers (handmade, Provo Craft); mini brads (Making Memories); monogram letters (K & Company); leather trim (Westrim); ribbon (Morex Corp.); mesh (Magic Mesh); cardstock; stamping inks

The **Labrador retriever**, **golden retriever** and **German shepherd** are first, second, and third on the American Kennel Club's list of **most popular dog breeds**.

# Precious Baby Bunnies

These precious bunnies were adopted into Mary's family from a bunny rescue, and their adorable cuddle-ability served as the inspiration for this two-page spread. Mary used powder blue for the background to make her photos pop and incorporated additional blue and orange papers to highlight the carrot shown in select images. She combined word charms with foam-stamped letters to form her title and added sheer polka-dot ribbons for finishing embellishments.

**Mary Litton, Holloman Air Force Base, New Mexico**

**Supplies:** Patterned papers (Basic Grey); foam letter stamps, decorative brads (Making Memories); metal word charm (Karen Foster Design); frosted word accent, rub-on letters (Doodlebug Design); metal word ribbon charm (K & Company); ribbons (May Arts); metal label holder (EK Success); acrylic paint; mini brads

# POOKIES AND SCAMPER

## PLAY

My husband really wanted to get a couple of dwarf hamsters for his birthday. I was skeptical and thought they would be more of a hassle than anything else. Well, it does take a lot of effort to clean the cages, but we have both really enjoyed them! We got two girls, a dark hamster named Pookies, and a tan one who we call Scamper. They are active little critters...when they're awake, they are constantly busy. They love to run in their exercise wheel, hoard and bury food, scurry around the habitrail, wrestle with each other, and eat. They keep us entertained and even make us laugh...I never thought little rodent beasts could be so funny. We've become good friends with them, and they like coming out of their cage daily so we can hold them.

March 2005

Most **hamsters** are solitary animals and should be **kept in separate cages** to avoid fighting.

## Pookies and Scamper

When Lorell's husband suggested they adopt a couple of dwarf hamsters, she never imagined how much fun the tiny rodents would be. For the larger photos of Pookies and Scamper, Lorell created segmented photo mats linked by white string. Several ink-edged word paper elements adorned with heart-shaped brads balance out the journaling block on the bottom of the spread, while round ribbon slides, round stamped title letters and a spiral clip elicit the kinesthetic fun of a hamster wheel.

**Lorell Rogers, Meridian, Idaho**

**Supplies:** Patterned paper, word paper elements (My Mind's Eye); textured cardstocks (Bazzill); letter stamps (Stampin' Up!); ribbon, heart brads, spiral clip (Making Memories); ribbon rounds (Junkitz); rub-on word (Li'l Davis Designs); fibers; string; stamping ink; foam adhesive spacers

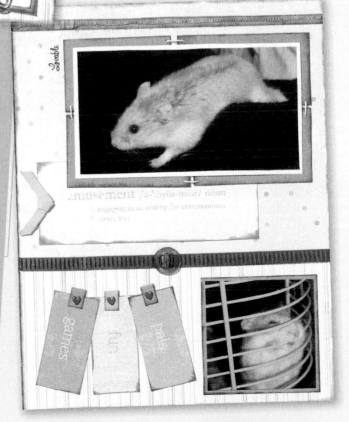

Lovable

amusement /ə-'myüz-mənt/ noun
1. engaging in an activity for entertainment
2. distraction

games    fun    pals

## Piper

The third prospective home proved to be a charm for Piper. From her litter, to another family and then into Diana's life, this perpetual ball of energy has found a permanent address and a best friend in Diana to boot! Vibrantly colored patterned paper helps to illustrate Piper's high-strung playfulness, while bright orange cardstock journaling and title elements continue the look of excitement and fun, complemented by brilliant blue accents.

**Diana McMillan, Fort Worth, Texas**

**Supplies:** Patterned paper (Design Originals); textured cardstock (Bazzill); ribbon (Making Memories); mini brads (Boxer Scrapbook Productions); die-cut letters (QuickKutz); stamping ink; foam adhesive spacers

## Amun

Kimberly's children desperately wanted a bright orange cat, and it didn't take long for the entire family to fall in love with this marmalade sweetheart they discovered at a pet store. Kimberly created this layout using photo-editing software to form a black-and-white background to contrast against Amun's vibrant fur. The label strip along the left reveals all the favorite "pet" names of this family's "orange little man."

**Kimberly Vogel, Gulfport, Mississippi**

**Supplies:** Patterned paper (Basic Grey); metal photo corners, foam letter stamps (Making Memories); label maker (Dymo); paint chip (Home Depot); image-editing software (Adobe Photoshop); label holder (source unknown); acrylic paint; brads; cardstock

# My Little Lion

Nearly 10 years later, Nicole still remembers the day she brought home her "Little Lion" from a local animal shelter, and created this page to celebrate him. She played up the circular design in her patterned paper by adding a border of cardstock circles featuring cropped images of her favorite feline. She painted her chipboard letters and letter stencil, and then polished off the look with sheer circular droplets of shine created with dimensional glaze.

Nicole Pereira, Santa Clara, California

**Supplies:** Patterned paper (Urban Lily); textured cardstock (Bazzill); letter stickers (Sticker Studio); rub-on letters (Autumn Leaves); chipboard letters (Making Memories); dimensional glaze (JudiKins); acrylic paint; stamping ink

MY LITTLE LION

About ten years ago, when I was fifteen, I told my mom I wanted a cat. She was reluctant because she knew cleaning the litter box was soon to become her job (and she was right), but in the end we still made a trip to the local animal shelter. I wanted an orange cat, but the only kitten ready to go was a white cat with orange spots. I wanted a cat so bad that those few spots of orange were sufficient. I named him Mango, because his spots reminded me of the color of mangos. He is such a sweet cat... well sometimes. He can be feisty and because he is slightly chunky, I often think of him as my little lion.

**Cats** are often thought to be *colorblind*, but recent studies have shown that cats can *see blue, green and red*.

## ...These Little Piggies...

Ashley's two-page spread tells the story of how two little piggies, given as gifts, suddenly became four little piggies, as each gift was suddenly discovered to be expecting! Ashley used a simplistic page design for this family affair, featuring a handcut curve for visual interest and neutral papers appropriate for both mama and baby guinea pigs. The ribbon-adorned patterned paper curve lifts to reveal Ashley's hidden journaling. White rub-on letters were applied directly onto each guinea pig's photo for comedic-looking captions.

**Ashley Calder, Dundas, Ontario, Canada**

**Supplies:** Patterned paper (Me & My Big Ideas); rub-on letters, ribbon (Chatterbox); metal heart charm (Jo-Ann Stores); solvent ink (Tsukineko); cardstock; pen.

Pearl and Miss Piggy were gifts to Summer Lily on her 3rd birthday. A few weeks later we realized chubby Miss Piggy was pregnant and then a few days after that – realized Pearl was too. In September Miss Piggy and then Pearl had their babies, a few days apart. Both mamas had complications in birthing and after several trips to a few different vets (many after hours), lots of phone calls to other vets all over Guelph and Hamilton, we ended up with one mama piggy Pearl to care after Miss Piggy's three babies. One of Miss Piggy's babies was born blind and deaf, due to a genetic problem (lethal white) and passed away about a week after he was born. We eventually named the two babies – Slick and Steve French. Pearl and the boys are living happily in our kitchen.... in seperate cages, of course.

photos September 2004. journalling April 2005.

**Guinea pigs** make great pets because they are **affectionate and social, inexpensive, require little space** and, unlike other rodents, do not smell because they do not have musk glands.

everything has beauty but not everyone sees it.

-confucius

January 2005 So... why do you have it? Sebastian is not your average pet. We get a lot of questions about him, and some very strong opinions. He's "creepy"... "scary"... "gross". But then you take a look into his eyes and you understand.

## Everything Has Beauty...

One look into the eyes of this "creepy" and "scary" hermit crab and he is quickly transformed into a precious thing of beauty. Melanie designed this 8 x 8" layout to share the shellshocked reactions people have had to her family's lovable pet and to illustrate how a soulful gaze like Sebastian's reveals his personality and the reasons why they adopted him in the first place. She found a 12 x 12" quote strip that suited the emotion of her page and trimmed it to size to fill the smaller format.

Melanie Howard, Saint-Joseph-du-lac, Quebec, Canada

**Supplies:** Patterned paper (Imagination Project); pen

## Fishies

You can almost hear the soothing sounds of water coming from Courtney's new 55-gallon fish tank, which she recently filled with brand-new, beautiful fish. Courtney used soft, subtle shades of papers and shimmering ribbon to complement the aquatic foliage and peacefulness of her aquarium. Even the overall page design resembles the look of a tank. To capture the crisp, clear photo of her fishes' new digs, Courtney used a Nikon D70 at a higher ISO and slower shutter speed.

Courtney Kelly, Colorado Springs, Colorado

**Supplies:** Patterned paper (Chatterbox); ribbon charm (source unknown); cardstock; ribbon

After dealing with too many issues with our 10 gallon tank we upgraded to a 55 gallon one. Of course with the larger tank allowed for more fish and Tom insisted that this wouldn't be a guppy tank. Unsatisfied with Petsmart, we found a local fish shop, and we've gotten some really beautiful fish, large, colorful, and not wimpy. I love to just sit there, especially at night, hearing the sounds of the water and just watching them, total relaxation at the end of a long day.

# Penny

The story of how Penny the puppy got her name (Diana's little girl saved up her own money) is journaled in fairy-tale format and set between shimmering copper ribbons to coordinate with the actual pennies adorning the layout. Diana printed the letters of Penny's name onto mosaic patterned paper, cut them out and matted them on cardstock. Each tile was set on a foam adhesive spacer for dimension, and black clips were added to tie in with Penny's coat.

Diana McMillan, Fort Worth, Texas

Supplies: Patterned papers, metal clips (Design Originals); textured cardstocks (Bazzill); ribbon (Offray); stamping ink; pennies

### The Story of Penny

Once upon a time there was a Princess in the land. Her name was Nikole. For the most part she was a happy little girl, but somehow she felt something was missing. She had a empty place in her heart that longed to be filled. She thought& thought- what could be missing. Then one day as she was playing in the court-yard it came to her. She went run-ning to the Queen. "Mommy, I want a puppy". The startled Queen quick-ly said, "You are to young for a puppy". The princess responded, "Oh I promise to take really good care of it! Please may I get a puppy?" The Queen said, "If you save up enough money you may get a puppy". Every day she helped out around the castle to earn extra money. After a few weeks she emp-tied out her piggy bank and scooped up the pennies and went to the queen and said, "Is this enough money yet mommy?" Finally the Princess saved up enough pennies to get her puppy. And thats how the new puppy got the name Penny.

1. Monthly question asked by son, "Mom when can we get a dog?" same reply monthly, "When you are 9 yrs. old. (Gives me 2 more years)

2. Husband brings home picture of friends' new bulldog puppy. (I know this is a setup, I have always wanted a bulldog)

3. Picture of the adorable puppy is placed in the basket, which I secretly pick up and adore a hundred times a day. (This is not looking good already)

4. I start to only LOOK at bulldog puppies for sell on the Internet, hopefully nobody catches me.

5. I have narrowed my search down to two puppies; I really hope the one is still available. (Bet you can the direction this plan is taking, geesh!)

6. Call the breeder, which is 4 hours away, JUST to inquire about the puppy. (Yep, slowly breaking at this point)

7. Show the puppy to hubby who states," If we get the puppy, you have to wait for Christmas for you D70 camera." Puppy or camera for birthday? (This is where I just get pathetic)

8. Five minutes later, back on the phone with the breeder, deposit is made; I leave in 2 days to pick up our new puppy.

9. Hurry to the pet store to buy all the essentials for the new puppy, well maybe a few non-essentials, but that is ok, we are getting a new puppy!

10. Secretly leave on the road trip to get new puppy, two youngest have no clue where I am going, I am so excited.

11. Arrive at the breeders home, my heart melts, just confirms I made the right decision.

12. Arrive back home, pull into driveway, open car door and watch one 7 year old boy's dream come true, a new puppy's.

## No! Dog

It was hard for Ruth to hold her ground against getting a puppy after her husband planted the seed in her heart with a mere photo of a baby bulldog. From there it was game over, as Ruth's journaling describes the 12-step transformation that went from a son's persistent begging to an entire family's constant joy. Ruth handcut the "no" symbol beneath her chipboard letter title and repeated the circle shape in a metal-rimmed framed photo of Bentley.

Ruth Halford, Conway, South Carolina

Supplies: Patterned papers (Junkitz); chipboard letters, ribbon, metal-rimmed tag (Making Memories); acrylic paint; transparency

## Pet Page Topics

- How your pet joined the family
- Adoption day or lineage
- Growth chart
- Personality traits
- Knowledge of commands, vocabulary and signals
- Special talents and tricks
- Favorite forms of play
- A day in the life
- House rules according to your pet
- Favorite possessions
- Holidays with your pet
- Pet birthdays
- Childhood/past pets

## Dixie

It was a grand reunion for Dixie the Siberian husky and her owners when they discovered their runaway dog alive after an entire month of searching. JoAnne created this page to document the amazing return of her parents' beloved "miracle," journaling the story on a pull-out card behind Dixie's photo. She used the dog's powder blue eyes and polka-dot collar as the inspiration for her paper and color selections.

JoAnne Bacon,
Alpharetta, Georgia

**Supplies:** Patterned papers, nailheads (Chatterbox); ribbon (Making Memories); silk flowers; cardstock; eyelet; stamping ink

Dixie is my mother's dog. Beautiful isn't she? She is a purebred Siberian husky and loves to run, especially when she's on her leash. One day, just after New Years, Mom was taking her for a walk when she pulled loose, her leash still attached. My parents looked for hours but to no avail. Sooner or later, they assumed she would find her way home. They notified the neighbors that she was missing and waited, knowing that Dixie would probably be gone for a few hours. Those few hours turned into days and those days turned into weeks. All efforts to locate her were exhausted. After three weeks my parents had come to the awful conclusion that possibly Dixie had gotten her leash hung up somewhere in the woods and died. Hopefully, if she was still alive, someone had taken her in; she was after all, a very sweet animal. It was about this time, almost a month after her disappearance, that Mom's four-year-old neighbor ran into her kitchen screaming that he had found something. Just down the street, tied very tightly to a tree was Dixie, thin and ragged but very happy to see my mother. She was wrapped so tightly the Mom had to cut her loose. They made an immediate trip to the vet and determined that she was malnourished (15 pounds thinner) and a little beat up but otherwise healthy. I haven't seen my parents as happy as they were that day in a long time. Their prayers were answered and they now call her their Miracle. February 2005

## Pepper

Finding a family was easy for Pepper—she simply showed up in Jen's garage and began ruling the household with an iron paw from that day forward! Jen emphasized Pepper's striking eyes with bold geometric shapes, using patterned paper with circles cut out to reveal coordinating patterns beneath. She lined up all boundaries of her layers of patterned paper to create a free-flowing, continuous design. For added visual interest, Jen sanded her title letter stickers as a subtle extra touch.

Jen Nichols, Orland, Indiana

**Supplies:** Patterned paper (Imagination Project); letter stickers (American Crafts, EK Success, Imagination Project); transparency; sandpaper

Frisky (frĭs'kē) adj. Energetic, lively, and playful.

Pepper is the cat who claimed us as her family. One day she just appeared in our garage and from that day forward she has ruled the household. She is the one all the other cats defer to. The older she gets the better behaved those other cats had better be. This cat will allow no messing around in her home. The others know that they must let her eat first or be prepared for a good hiss and slap. There should be no notion of sharing a lap or a bed if she is already there. Make no mistake this family's home belongs to Pepper!

Trust (trŭst) n. Firm reliance on the integrity, ability, or character of a person or thing.

**WHISKERS** (whĭs'kərs) n. Long projecting hairs or bristles that grow near the mouth of an animal.

PEPPER

2005

We have had BUSTER for over 11 years. He was given to us by my father and is an Australian Cattle dog. BUSTER has always lived in a dog-pen that we built for him. As he got older, we would let him stay out during the day in our yard. During a thunderstorm last August, BUSTER disappeared. We searched all over town for him but to no avail. Imagine our surprise when he was found six months later! Town workers found a dog nearly dead and recognized him as our dog. We took him to the vet's where he stayed for over two weeks. BUSTER had nearly starved to death. He was so weak he could not stand or walk. BUSTER is so glad to be home and we are so glad to have him home. The funny thing now is he won't hardly leave his dog-pen. If he could talk, I am sure he would repeat over and over..."there's no place like home!!!!!"

## Buster's Saga

"There's no place like home" has become Buster's mantra. After disappearing from Beverly's home during a thunderstorm, this nearly 12-year-old furry family member was found half-starved SIX months later! Beverly shares the amazing story on Buster's page, designed with the look of a hero's welcome. Muted shades of red, white and blue express celebration of the brave dog's return home, while stapled striped ribbons add a dynamic touch to the design.

**Beverly Sizemore, Sulligent, Alabama**

**Supplies:** Patterned paper, rub-on letters, round tags, tabs, brads (SEI); die-cut tags and letters (Sizzix); word stamp (Leave Memories); letter stamps (Creative Imaginations); number stamps (Hero Arts); ribbon (Great Balls of Fiber); colored staples (Making Memories); circle punch (Marvy); vellum; foam adhesive spacers; embossing powder; stamping ink

The *United States* and *France* have the **most pet dogs,** with **one in three families** owning a dog. Germany and Switzerland have the fewest, with only one in 10 families owning dogs.

## Protector

While working at a local sheltie rescue group after the loss of her first sheltie, Lisa fell in love with George, her loyal protector and hero. This warm layout boasts brown painted elements that add a touch of masculinity, including the title treatment, chipboard photo corners and jigsaw letter. Lisa wrote her journaling on small cards tucked inside a coin envelope that rests behind the lower accent photo. Pet-themed paper, stickers and whimsical dog bone embellishments add nearly as much charm to this page as George himself.

Lisa Turley, Chesapeake, Virginia

Supplies: Patterned paper, cardstock stickers, metal tags (Flair Designs); textured cardstock, coin envelope (Bazzill); title letters (Sarah Heidt Photo Craft); bone clips, mini brads (Creative Impressions); ribbon (May Arts); chipboard letters (Making Memories); chipboard; acrylic paint; pen.

## I Choose You

Kirsten's layout features the very first photo ever taken of her golden retriever puppy, Berkeley, and the instant bond she formed with Kirsten and her boyfriend. The bright color scheme gives the page a soft and sweet sense of excitement, embellished with sheer pink polka-dot ribbon for the finesse of a new baby girl. Kirsten inked the edges of her papers for contrast and set a paw print punch in the corner for puppy pizazz.

**Kirsten Dauphin, Denver, Colorado**

**Supplies:** Patterned paper (Daisy D's); textured cardstock (Bazzill); ribbon (May Arts); foam letter stamp (Li'l Davis Designs); decorative brad (Making Memories); chipboard letters (Li'l Davis Designs, Making Memories); woven label (Me & My Big Ideas); paw print punch (EK Success); acrylic paint; stamping ink

## Sisters

Not one, but two pug sisters are the apples of Joe's eye, as this layout testifies in celebration of their recent adoption into his heart and home. Joe loves to incorporate unique finds into his scrapbooks, and included a pug charm found while on vacation in Japan to represent a dog tag on the 3-D collar sticker. He personalized the page for his two "dogters" by engraving each of their names on a dog bone metal tag and attaching them to their corresponding framed portraits. He also created his own metal-rimmed tag accents by printing an assortment of fonts onto a transparency and adhering them behind die-cut circles.

**Joe Huber, Port Richey, Florida**

**Supplies:** Patterned paper (Flair Designs); textured cardstock (DieCuts with a View); ribbons (American Crafts); 3-D collar sticker (K & Company); twill tabs, metal frames (Making Memories); pug charm (found); letter stamps (Hero Arts); bone tags (Boxer Scrapbook Productions); distress ink (Ranger); engraving tool (Magic Scraps); metal-rimmed circle die-cut (Sizzix); marker; transparency

a faithful friend

special

*sweet!*

Cassidy is the sweetest dog that I know. We were so lucky to have found her. I called everywhere looking for a female yellow lab. No one had any in the area! My sister-in-law mentioned a place in Halstead that some of her friends had gotten their dogs from. After two months of searching, I was happy to try, even though it was in a different state. I left a message and began my wait. Two weeks later, she called, and said she had what I was looking for! Cassidy was the only female from a litter of seven. She said she was going to keep her to show, then changed her mind. I asked what she was like. She replied " She is so sweet, calm and pretty." I told her I would take her! I have to say that even today, Cassidy is exactly what the breeder had described and better! I couldn't have asked for a better dog. She is one of the family and the favorite among the neighborhood. Her favorite activity is eating. She loves kids and other dogs. Not to mention the smartest animal I have ever encountered. I feel she was always meant to be with us. We love her so!

## Cassidy

When Cari was searching for a female yellow lab pup to join her family, the breeder described Cassidy as "sweet, calm and pretty," as is reflected in the look and feel of this tribute page. Cari loved the way the image of Cassidy stood out from the textured background of this serene photo, so she continued the visual textures onto the layout using layers of distressed-looking patterned papers with torn and inked edges. A monogram letter and letter stickers set along a ribbon accent spell out Cari's faithful friend's name, while painted metal plaques help describe her character.

Cari Fennell, Dewitt, New York

**Supplies:** Patterned papers (Basic Grey, Pebbles); monogram letter, letter stickers (Basic Grey); ribbon (May Arts); metal word charms, mini brads (Making Memories); distress ink (Ranger); acrylic paint; transparency

## Family of 4

Since Renae's cats are such an important part of her household, she designed this layout to feature all four of these furry family members together. Images of each feline are artfully arranged on the left, balanced by a chipboard frame enhanced by rub-on letters and a pet-themed charm. Renae's journaling block describes how her family acquired each cat and reveals several personality traits and favorite pastimes each enjoys.

Renae Clark, Mazomanie, Wisconsin

**Supplies:** Patterned papers, number sticker, sticker strips, metal fish charm (Flair Designs); textured cardstock (Bazzill); chipboard frame (Li'l Davis Designs); rub-on letters (Kopp Design); ribbon (May Arts); corner rounder (Creative Memories)

WILD THING VITTLES · CATNIP · ZOOM OST · SUN SPOT · YOWL · WHISKERS

Over the years our family of felines has grown to four. *Gizmo*, has been a part of our family for 9 years. She is very shy & tends to bounce around the house more at night after the boys are sleeping. She also like to snuggle with Tanner. *Tasha* came to us from the Angel's Wish Foundation. She was an abandon cat. She is very set in her ways & has habits she just can't break. For example, as soon as Daenon hits the sack, she hops up on his bed & snuggles in next to him. She also waits for him at the door to arrive home from school. *Shelly*, our 3rd kitty also comes from an abandon animal shelter. She was an orphan for six months & we can't figure out why. She is such a sweet lovable kitty that will share a love bite with you. Our fourth cat, *Dexter*, was literally found on our Deck. (Thus, the reason we named her Dex (the dock cat!). When we happened upon her she was starving & very frail from malnutrition. We started leaving food on the deck for her & she would come every night for dinner and a few pettings. It took several months for her to warm up to us, but she now enjoys living in the comforts of our home 24 hours a day. We have grown into a family of cat lovers & we enjoy all four members of our feline family!

FAMILY OF

4

Meow

Tabby · Kitty Crazies · Meow Tail · cat food · cuddly · co

## A Dog's Life

Although her heart had been set on bringing home a Siberian husky pup, once Nikki laid eyes on Zazu, a chow, it was love at first sight. Nikki's journaling tells the story of the day she brought home her "baby bear cub" and the emotional roller coaster involved. The blue patterned paper serves as a complement to Zazu's golden fur, while photos printed on textured cardstock create the look of canvas. Nikki softened the look of the page with shimmering ribbon adhered to the photo tag accentuated by mini tags held by colorful safety pins.

Nikki Hobbs, Nampa, Idaho

**Supplies:** Patterned paper (Daisy D's); textured cardstock (Bazzill); ribbon (American Crafts, www.lifetime moments.com); wooden tag, rub-on letters (Chatterbox); letter stickers (American Crafts); mini brads (Lasting Impressions); letter buttons (Junkitz); safety pins, mini tags (Making Memories); letter stamps (MoBe' Stamps!); stamping ink

MAR 2005

Zazu is a big part of my life. I remember the day we brought him home. We had just moved in to our new house on Brooklyn Ave, I was in 10th grade (1994-95). My parents took my sister and I to Andy's Pet shop. I had my heart set on getting an alaskan malamute or siberian Husky, so I could name him Nanook after the dog in one of my all time favorite movies "LOST BOYS". Both my sister and I picked two siberian Huskys. My mom approached me a couple minutes later. She said she knew I had my heart set on the Husky, but she wanted me to see another dog. So I followed her over to a pen that held a couple of Chow Chows. As soon as I saw them I knew I was inlove! They looked like baby bear cubs. I had the hardest time picking between the two brothers. They looked like twins. I finally picked. I left that store with a brokenheart, I wish we could have gotten them both, we even tried to get my sister to get the brother chow, but her heart was set on the Husky. I ended up naming my Chow dog after the hornbill bird from the disney movie "The Lion King", I was going to name him mufasa (The Lion King) but my dad said it would be to hard for him to remember lol, so ZAZU it was.

The **chow chow and Shar-Pei** are unique dog breeds for their **blue-black tongues.** Other animals that share this trait are the giraffe, polar bear and select breeds of cattle.

Pet is an aqua frog. Mitchell got her for Christmas in 2001. This little animal has out lasted all other pets that we have had. We tried a puppy when the kids were 1 and 3. All that puppy wanted to do was heard the kids and nip at their heals. Chessapeak only lasted a month. Next came our cat Shadow. We loved her very much and planned on having her for a very long time but she got sick after almost a year, and died. Then came our cat Sandy who we adopted. Little did we know that people could be allergic to just some cats. Mitchell and I were both allergic to Sandy. Off she went to another good home. Then came the hermit crab named Lobster. We added a second hermit crab to his cage after returning home from vacation, not sure if he ever got named since his claw fell off and he died within a week of his arrival. Lobster didn't meet up with his roommate until a few months later. We were given a beautiful red Beta Fish and Alayna named her Lipstick. She did great until we put her in with Penelope and she died within a week. Oh and can't forget about Penelopes temporary roommates Gary the snail and another snail with no name. They too failed to live a long and fulfilled life. But just when we think we are a plague to our pets, there is Penelope who has been with us for a year and a half now. It isn't promising knowing that her life expectancy is about 2 years, but we hope to have her around for a long time.

# Penelope

Kim chose cheerful, unconventional colors to complement the personality of Penelope, the aqua frog, who has outlived all the other pets in the family! To help the images of this life-affirming amphibian stand out in the photos, Kim created a decorative arrow for one and used a letter "o" foam stamp to point her out in the other. In order to make her journaling more legible over the vibrant patterned paper, she transitioned the text color from pink to black. A beaded frog sticker set on a dancing-letter title provides the perfect touch for pulling the whimsical page together.

Kim Hughes, Roy, Utah

**Supplies:** Patterned paper (Scrapworks); textured cardstock (Bazzill); foam letter stamps, brads, button, chipboard letters (Making Memories); ribbon (American Crafts); beaded frog sticker (SEI); rub-on letter (Me & My Big Ideas); metal-rimmed circle word (K & Company); number stickers (Bo-Bunny Press); transparency; silk flowers

The **largest species of frog** resides in West Africa and can **grow up to 15 inches** and **weigh up to 7 pounds.** The smallest is a species of **Cuban frog** that only **grows to less than ½" long.**

## He'll Get How Big?

Courtney's family has a history of owning large dogs, but her brother's bull mastiff, Peyton, is gigantic! She designed this page to preserve the memory of Peyton as a cuddly little pup before he grew into an enormous dog. Courtney stapled folds of ribbon, fabric and fibers to form a border along the bottom of the page, playing up the soft side of this gentle giant while coordinating with the colors in the plaid patterned paper. Chipboard letters lend a touch of sturdy strength, suiting Peyton perfectly.

**Courtney Walsh, Winnebago, Illinois**

**Supplies:** Patterned paper, photo corners, number stickers (Chatterbox); chipboard letters (Li'l Davis Designs, Making Memories); ribbon (May Arts, Michaels, M&J Trimming); fabric (Junkitz); metal-rimmed tags (Avery); cardstock; acrylic paint; stamping ink; gel pen

## Soda

Pure, unbridled bliss is captured in the expression of Ronnie's son, James, in the midst of bringing home the family's new puppy. Ronnie's computer-generated layout combines a cheery red background with a bold circular design, which is shaded in a hue reminiscent of a golden retriever's coat and accentuated with a collar, ribbons and letter stencil elements. Since the puppy was named Soda, Ronnie appropriately used a bottle cap to add a little pizazz to the title lettering.

**Ronnie McCray, St. James, Missouri**

**Supplies:** Bottle cap (Dorothy Gibson, Computer Scrapping Elements 2 Yahoo Group); dog collar (Ronnie McCray Dog kit, www.pagesoftheheart.net); tiny jewelry tag (Ronnie McCray Make Time Stand Still kit, www.pagesoftheheart.net); flower brush (Ronnie McCray Rugged Outdoors kit, www.pagesoftheheart.net); remaining digital elements (artists own design)

# Heidi

Ginger's children's persistent begging paid off, resulting in the adoption of this sweet Cavalier King Charles Spaniel named Heidi. Ginger's journaling tells her change-of-heart story of instantly becoming a "dog person" once she laid eyes on this precious pup. Ginger used brown, pet-themed papers and brown stamping ink to complement the sepia images, all of which proved to be perfect touches for this page commemorating this sweet new arrival.

**Ginger McSwain, Cary, North Carolina**

**Supplies:** Patterned paper (Boxer Scrapbook Productions); ribbon (Michaels); paw print stamp (All Night Media); stamping ink; textured cardstock; circle punch

Meet Heidi. Heidi is our new little puppy and the result of 2 years of begging by Rachel and Samuel. I have never owned a dog before. I have never wanted to own a dog before. I have never considered my self a 'dog person' before. So, why is it that this little Cavalier King Charles Spaniel has completely stolen my heart? I told myself that I was doing this for the kids... that I could sacrifice my time and the attention that a new dog would require not to mention the extra work and cost she would entail... all for the two of them. Little did I know that I would immediately love her as much as both Rachel and Samuel love her. She is the perfect pet for us. She is worth the extra work and sacrifices. She is our Heidi.

# The Story of Dodger Our Turtle...

While trying to cross a busy highway during a rainstorm, Dodger the turtle found higher ground in the arms of Pam's husband, who pulled their car off the road to rescue him. To tell Dodger's story, Pam kept the page design simple, using distressed-effect patterned papers in different shapes to play up the colors and texture of Dodger's shell, while copper mini brads mimic the orange markings of his neck and legs.

**Pam Sivage, Georgetown, Texas**

**Supplies:** Patterned papers, letter stickers (Basic Grey); textured cardstock (Bazzill); date stamp (Making Memories); brads

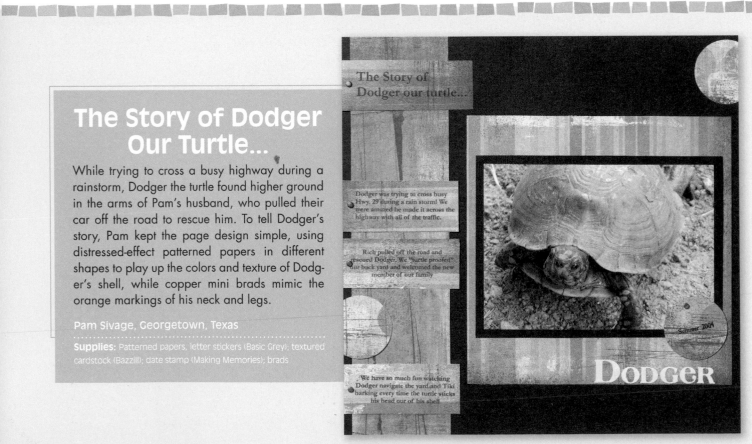

The Story of Dodger our turtle...

Dodger was trying to cross busy Hwy. 29 during a rain storm! We were amazed he made it across the highway with all of the traffic.

Rich pulled off the road and rescued Dodger. We "turtle proofed" our back yard and welcomed the new member of our family

We have so much fun watching Dodger navigate the yard and Tiki barking every time the turtle sticks his head out of his shell

Summer 2004

DODGER

## Farley 2004

In the world of dog sports, dogs become "veterans" in their careers at the age of 8. This majestic pose of Farley in the leaves was a great way for Mary to commemorate this Frisbee-champ's eighth birthday and to reminisce on his adoption and many achievements thus far. Mary designed this computer-generated masterpiece utilizing brushes downloaded from the Internet and custom designs she developed herself.

Mary Hager, Bainbridge Island, Washington

Supplies: Image-editing software (Adobe Photoshop CS); brushes (downloaded from Internet and custom-designed)

frisbee

agility

obedience

You came to us under special circumstances – a rescue given up by your previous family. Little did they know what an incredible dog you would turn out to be. Personally, I am glad they gave you up, because if they had realized your potential, I would not have had the past 5 years with you.

On this birthday, you will turn eight years old, and enter the fall of your life. In the past years, you have been my partner, my friend, and my once-in-a-lifetime dog. There is nothing you can not do, and no matter what task I give you, you do it with zeal and enthusiam.

You are my aussie, my agility dog, my obedience dog, my frisbee partner and my family member. I am looking forward to more competitions, more wins and hopefully many more years with you.

*Farley*

2N O o O v 4

Farley's Titles: OAC, NGC, EJC, QA, OAJ, CD.
1st Place Phoenix Skyhoundz Disc Dog 2002, 2nd Place 2001

# Rusty
## our new puppy

One unregistered yellow lab puppy = $25

Doghouse, dog food and supplies = $200

The smile on Preston's face = PRICELESS

## Rusty: Our New Puppy

Happiness truly is a warm puppy, as is evident on the face of Preston, snuggling up to his adorable new yellow lab. Jackie created a price tag to adhere to the large photo on the left page, with words inspired by a popular commercial. She added photo corners for a timeless touch and ran a band of gingham ribbon from the left page to the right to tie the spread together. The right page lists the life lessons one can learn from a dog, with precious photos on the far right to highlight this new family friend.

Jackie Pettit, Morgan, Utah

**Supplies:** Textured cardstock (Bazzill); letter stickers (Creative Imaginations); ribbon, date stamp (Making Memories); solvent ink (Tsukineko); acrylic bone charm (Doodlebug Design); die-cut letters (QuicKutz); photo corners (Canson)

Yellow lab puppies come in *18 shades of yellow*.

### Things We Can Learn From a Dog

Never pass up the opportunity to go for a joy ride.

Allow the experience of fresh air and the wind in your face to be pure ecstasy.

When loved ones come home, always run to greet them.

When it's in your best interest, practice obedience.

Let others know when they've invaded your territory.

Take naps and stretch before rising.

Run, romp, and play daily.

Eat with gusto and enthusiasm.

Be loyal.

Never pretend to be something you're not.

If what you want lies buried, dig until you find it.

When someone is having a bad day, be silent, sit close by and nuzzle them gently.

Thrive on attention and let people touch you.

On hot days, drink lots of water and lie under a shady tree.

When you're happy, dance around and wag your entire body.

No matter how often you're scolded, don't buy into the guilt thing and pout run right back and make friends.

Delight in the simple joys of a long walk.

---author unknown

January 2004

The **most intelligent breeds of dogs** are said to be the *border collie*, the *poodle* and the *golden retriever*.

## Pitter-Patter of Puppy Paws

Just when the Richardsons thought no more children were on the horizon, this sweet, furry baby brought the pitter-patter of puppy paws into their home to complete their family. JD incorporated close-up images of Ginger's paws into the mosaic of textural tiles. She used a paw print stamp on numerous squares for the look of doggy steps over a kitchen floor, and embossed several with gold powder to coordinate with the metallic papers. Using a monogram letter and rub-on letters, she formed a large title tile on chipboard, accenting it with twill and ribbons, all set on foam adhesive spacers for depth.

JD Richardson, Saint John, New Brunswick, Canada

**Supplies:** Textured papers (Emagination Crafts, Magic Scraps, Provo Craft, Wintech); chipboard monogram (Heidi Swapp); heart charm (Making Memories); paw print stamp (Whispers); twill (Maya Road); ribbon (Offray); rub-on letters, letter stamps (source unknown); tag (Avery); distress inks (Ranger); embossing powder

## Sophie

**The unexpected puppy**

We didn't really know that we were about to get a new puppy. January 2nd, 2005, we woke up like any other day, unsuspecting of the plan that Victoria and Abuelo were hatching...

by the end of the day, we were the proud owners of the cutest Papillon puppy ever! We were unsure what to name her, and tried name after name, but none seemed to fit (Sunshine was a strong contender). Finally, Craig came up with the perfect name for a little French dog: Sophie.

Victoria loved it, and she added Madeleine as a middle name, just in case we ever needed to yell at the puppy if she misbehaved ☺

It turns out that she misbehaves a lot, but we haven't used her middle name just yet. So far, we are all too busy just loving her to notice any messes or bad habits on her part.

01·05

Victoria says

Nicholas says

Carbon says

She is mine. She is all mine, my dear puppy is here at last.

I got me a puppy.

When is this obnoxious puppy going home?

## Sophie

This adorable papillon puppy was an unexpected addition to Maria's family, but no one can say enough about how lovable little Sophie turned out to be. Maria used a long journaling block accentuated with bold black rickrack to keep the layout clean and crisp, while vibrant colors help capture this pup's personality. Maria added die-cut matchbooks to hold the journaling of each of her children, revealing their own personal reflections on this much-loved, furry friend.

Maria Gallardo-Williams, Cary, North Carolina

**Supplies:** Patterned paper (Scraps and Scribbles); rickrack, ribbon (Offray); chipboard letter (Li'l Davis Designs); die-cut matchbooks (Legacy Paper Arts); letter stickers (Chatterbox, EK Success, unknown); cardstock; pen

## Photo Checklist

- Individual pet "parts"
- Stages of growth
- Showing off tricks
- A day in the life
- Bath time
- Sleeping
- At play
- Getting into trouble
- Before and after grooming
- Favorite around-the-house spots
- Veterinary visits
- Trips to the park
- Favorite toys

# My Girl

Sherry's journaling expresses her feelings and love for her best friend with a tail, who has helped her grow from a young woman in college to a working mother, sharing in every sorrow and joy along the way. To dress up her feminine design, Sherry adhered a soft fabric accent to A'Keyla's portrait and a stamped image on the upper right corner of the photo to give her pooch a prestigious air and to coordinate with the printed transparency along the bottom. Paper flowers sprinkled about the page help unify the overall look of simplistic beauty.

Sherry Wright, West Branch, Michigan

**Supplies:** Patterned paper, printed transparency, epoxy stickers (Autumn Leaves); textured cardstock (Bazzill); paper flowers (Prima); fabric accent (EK Success); letter stamps (Ma Vinci's Reliquary); decorative trim (Wrights); foam corner stamp (Making Memories); die-cut letter (Sizzix); label maker (Dymo); transparency; stamping ink

SUN CATCHER

Let the sun fall on your face, and the shadows will always fall behind you.
- Charlotte Whitton

Cosmo

He loves the sun. He bathes in it as though it were a warm pool of water. He rolls around...writhing as if he's trying to cover every strand of fur in the liquid gold. Then, when he's decided every square inch of him is thoroughly saturated...he sleeps...a big melted puddle of cat.

2005

# chapter two | Animal Behavior

Pets look at each moment of life as an opportunity to enjoy, no holds barred, and remind us to do the same. When your own complicated life becomes overwhelmed with unnecessary stresses, look to the example of your pet to be reminded that it's the simple things that bring the most sublime joy: a regular meal, a treat or two, a walk in the park, a comfy sleeping spot, a well-loved toy and human companionship. Pages of your pet enraptured in all things animal are sure to bring a smile to your face. So capture your favorite comrades in action every chance you get—even if it is while they're taste-testing your designer footwear or stealing some z's on the good couch.

## Kitty in a Basket

Any place is a great place for a catnap, according to Amy's kitty, Missy. When Amy found her asleep in this Ikea basket, she knew a page was in the works. Amy wanted the look of a word puzzle on this warm-colored design and came up with the idea of placing the words within brackets to mimic the image in the photo. To give the layout a hint of depth, she layered the photo and journaling on chipboard and added flower buttons for feminine feline flair.

Amy Smith, Los Angeles, California

**Supplies:** Patterned papers (Chatterbox); flower buttons (JHB International); chipboard

Sweet little Missy. Her tiny little self asleep in her basket. This kitty can take a cat nap anywhere. She'll find a cozy little area in the sun, curl up and bask for hours. From my pillow, to the top of the hope chest by the window, to this Ikea basket, she is never at a loss for that perfect snooze spot.

Cats are only awake 4-5 hours a day.

## Elliott on Guard

Susan's protective pooch, Elliott, guards the food bowl on this page dedicated to dog defense mechanisms. Susan machine-stitched blocks of patterned paper behind this comical photo and added stitched ribbon as well. A band of decorative vellum along the bottom softens the busy look of the patterns and heightens the contrast of the title letters. A slit cut in the patterned paper on the right provides a home for the journaling tag, which shares Elliott's hilarious behavior in detail.

Susan Wyno, Puyallup, Washington

**Supplies:** Patterned papers (Chatterbox, MOD- my own design, Scenic Route Paper Co.); patterned vellum (SEI); textured cardstock (Bazzill); ribbons (Michaels); chipboard letters (Li'l Davis Designs, Making Memories), label maker (Dymo); rub-on flowers (source unknown)

You don't want to eat your food, Elliott, yet you insist on guarding your bowl and growling at Mochi as long as there is anything left in it. I wish you'd just eat it or get over it!
4/2005

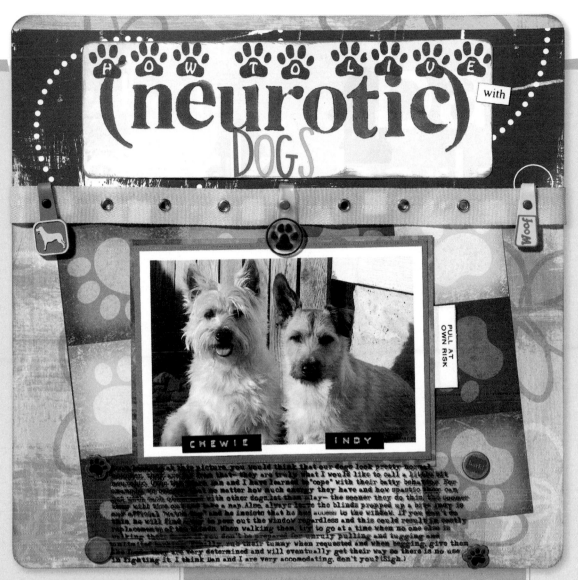

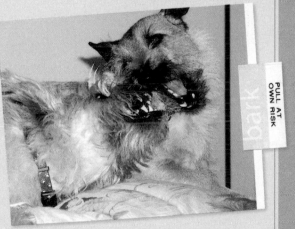

## How to Live With (Neurotic) Dogs

They may look like your average, adorable dogs, but these two can go from "normal" to "neurotic" in no time. Janetta's fun layout details the demanding behavior of Chewie and Indy, and includes a pull-out photo element and journaling that testifies to how these dogs punish their owners if they are not accommodated fully. The eyelet ribbon along the top serves as a dog collar embellishment and is adorned with rubberlike tags. Paw print letter stamps and magnetic pet-themed accents create a look that is far from "normal" but that is oh so fun!

**Janetta Abucejo Wieneke, Memory Makers Books**

**Supplies:** Patterned paper (Around The Block, Junkitz); letter stamps (Magnetic Poetry, Stamping Sensations); ribbon, rubber tag embellishments, brads, rub-on letters (Junkitz); magnetic word (Magnetic Poetry); dog-themed brads (Around The Block); label maker labels (Dymo); transparency (Grafix); corner rounders (EK Success); stamping ink; acrylic paint; foam adhesive spacers

# Incognito

Will the real kitty please stand up? She may be able to fool people with her majestic-looking outward appearances, but Mimi is convinced her cat Abby is actually a human toddler in disguise! She designed this page to record the true personality of her mischievous feline "child," listing many of the hilarious shenanigans of this innocent-looking beauty. Mimi machine-stitched around the border of her wavy patterned paper, carrying the design onto the cardstock. She also found a great way to use up leftover letter stickers by making tiny dots with the tops of i's and j's, and decorative circle elements with leftover o's.

Mimi Schramm, Colton, California

**Supplies:** Patterned paper (My Mind's Eye); textured cardstock (Bazzill); letter stickers (American Crafts, Creative Imaginations, Doodlebug Design, Wordsworth); foam letter stamp (Making Memories); thread; acrylic paint

Oh, she may look regal, dignified and sometimes majestic. She may even look like a cat. But, don't let her outward appearances fool you. What we have here is **a human toddler in disguise.**

One who once licked the frosting off a birthday cake when no one was looking.

One who thinks she is the most important "person" in the house.

One who cries incessantly for attention the minute I stop vacuuming.

One who likes to sleep on my pillow.

One who steals tissues from tissue boxes and unrolls toilet paper rolls.

One who plays with David's toys when everyone is in bed.

Yes, we have a **toddler.** She is of the feline variety and her name is **ABBY!**

# The Life of Jaxx

Michelle can't decide whether it's love or the pursuit of treats that causes Jaxx's daily ritual of dog-play to be followed by adoring gazes and cuddling. Michelle created this page to express her love for Jaxx and their special time together. The unique close-up photo of Jaxx puts the viewer into the heart of playtime, while framed accent photos illustrate the other joys of this dog's life. Slanted journaling elements inked with brown lend a rough and tumble feeling to the page.

Michelle Jacknicke, St. Albert, Alberta, Canada

**Supplies:** Patterned paper (Basic Grey); mini frames, ribbons (SEI); colored staples (Making Memories); cardstock; stamping ink

5:50 am - yes that's the morning! Sleepily raise head from the bed as Trent gets up.
6:00 am - wait for Trent to sit with his breakfast and then head to the door to whine to go outside
6:05 am - go back to bed
7:45 am - lift head again as the alarm goes off for the kids to go to school. Put head back down and go back to sleep
8:45 am - stagger out of the bedroom as everyone is heading out the door for school in hopes of going for a car ride
9:00 am - return home and back to bed
10:00 am - move from the bed to the couch
11:00 am - move from the couch to the floor
11:01 am - move from the floor back to the couch, being hit by too many hockey pucks or balls or toy of choice
11:35 am - another car ride to pick the kids up for lunch
11:50 am - home for lunch. hide in the bedroom so the kids won't sit on me
12:30 - stagger out of the bedroom again to take the kids back to school
12:50 - find a comfy spot on the couch
1:00 - move to the floor and find a sunny spot.
2:00 - walk by food dish. the grub is still there. boring.
3:20 - off we go again to get the kids from school
3:40 - retreat back to the bedroom. no target practice needed
4:40 - bark. jump at front door. bark some more. run to front window. bark. add a little whine in here and repeat (Trent is home)
5:15 - sit and drool as everyone eats supper and dog dish is topped off with the same old stuff.
6:30 - go for a walk. make sure to find all the puddles. bark at all other dogs. cower when they come near.
7:30 - find a spot on the couch if there is one.
8:00 - check out food dish. nibble on food. it's not as good as what everyone else was eating
10:30 - head to bed. it's been a ruff day!

## A Day in the Life

Another day, another bowl of the same boring dog food for this lovable family member, whose daily routine is humorously revealed on this clean and simple page. Kerry had fun describing in detail her pooch's "ruff day" in a way that perfectly suited the ho-hum expression captured in the photo. She used subtly patterned papers to help keep the endearing photo larger than life. A button centered in a silk flower accent lends feminine beauty, while the matted sticker works as a colorful embellishment as well as a title.

Kerry Zerff, Regina, Saskatchewan, Canada

**Supplies:** Patterned paper, textured cardstock (DieCuts with a View); phrase sticker (Pebbles); button, thread (Hillcreek Designs); silk flower

## Rules

what's wrong with this picture? if i've told you once, i've told you a million times — STAY OFF THE SCREEN! you're very intelligent, but i think you flunked listening skills class somewhere along the line. that, and sometimes you decide that rules are not made for you to follow. i know that you were simply curious as to what i was doing outside on the deck and trying to get a better view of life outside, but no excuses! keep your furry mitts off the screen or the door will remain closed. how's that for a threat?

# RULES

Caught red-pawed, Melanie's cat knows very well to stay off the screen door, but, as demonstrated on this page, often opts to break the rules. Melanie used the hilarious photo of her ornery-acting cat as the focus of this layout and balanced it with a journaling passage that serves as a loving, yet firm, parental advisory. She used patterned papers to draw out the green in Thomas' eyes and golds to play up his fur.

Melanie Bauer, Columbia, Missouri

**Supplies:** Patterned paper (Scenic Route Paper Co.); pen; stamping ink

## Bear

Bear can often be found waiting in eager anticipation for Kim's father-in-law to arrive home from work, as shown in these photos. Kim found this poem to be the perfect fit for her computer-generated creation about her in-laws' loyal pet, especially since they are gardeners as well. To create the paw print stamp, Kim used the animal tracks dingbat font for thematic effect and whimsy.

Kim Mauch, Portland, Oregon

**Supplies:** Image-editing software (Adobe Photoshop Elements); digital papers, elements (www.shabbyprincess.com)

bear

Somewhere a little dog doth wait;
It may be by some garden gate.
With eyes alert and tail attent—
You know the kind of tail that's meant
With stores of yelps of glad delight
To bid me welcome home at night.
—John Kendrick Bangs

## Beg

The title of Melanie's layout is two-fold: to chronicle the endearing look her cat Thomas bestows when begging for food, and also as a plea on her part for Thomas to refrain since no one can refuse him! Melanie used an elongated, vertical journaling block bordered by orange stripes to balance out the diagonal stripes in the photo, and created visual excitement through colorful circles cut from patterned paper and highlighted with a concho, brad and letter stickers.

**Melanie Bauer, Columbia, Missouri**

**Supplies:** Patterned paper (Scenic Route Paper Co.); textured cardstock (Bazzill); letter stickers (American Crafts); mini brad (Lasting Impressions); concho (Scrapworks); stamping ink; pen

## Caspurr

The striking yellow eyes of Miranda's feline set against his stark black fur are an eerily dynamic combo in this photo and seem to match the brilliant color of the grass in the background. Rather than create a layout overpowered with black to draw out her cat's fur, Miranda played up the vibrant green and generously inked each detail. The green worked well in setting a relaxed vibe on the page as well, meshing with this cat's cool attitude.

**Miranda Isenberg, Walled Lake, Michigan**

**Supplies:** Patterned paper, tags, frames (KI Memories); printed transparency (Artistic Expressions); textured cardstock, mini brads (Bazzill); rub-on letters (Making Memories); ribbon; staples; stamping ink; pen

## Salad Bar

While most guinea pigs are happy with a carrot and some chow, Debi's pampered piggies enjoy gourmet dining on a regular basis. Debi designated her design space for showcasing her guinea pigs' healthy eating habits by creating a grid with blocks of patterned paper, journaling and photos. She chose vibrant colors and shapes to create a smorgasbord of visual delight with garden-fresh appeal. A single acrylic ribbon slide on a strip of paper beneath the title adds just the right finishing touch.

Debi Boler, Newport Beach, California

**Supplies:** Patterned paper, acrylic ribbon slide (KI Memories); textured cardstock (Bazzill); corner rounder

## Waiting for a Big Adventure

Bretzen the little dachshund likes to behave boldly from behind the window while watching the world go by. Tricia documents how her little lady loves barking at rabbits and other trespassers while spectating from this spot inside. She gave her layout a playful look with vibrant colors and whimsically adorned tags. For a fun touch, she included a tape measure element to play off what she desicrbes as Bretzen's "small dog complex," or desire to act bigger and badder than her size would suggest!

Tricia Rubens, Castle Rock, Colorado

**Supplies:** Patterned paper; large shipping tag; rub-on letters; letter stamps (Rusty Pickle); bottle cap, bottle cap stickers (Design Originals); stickers (EK Success); label maker (Dymo); photo corners (Canson); tag punch (Emagination Crafts); die-cut tag toppers (Quickutz); stamps (Postmodern Design, Stampabilities, Stampington and Co.); ribbon (Offray); charms (7 Gypsies, Daisy D's, Yvonne Albrighton); embroidery floss, stamping ink

Max and Sara's relationship is such a funny one. They are the best of **friends**. They **play** with each other all the time, **chasing** each other around the house. They often take **naps** together. And I sometimes catch them **cleaning** each other. I have never seen a **cat** and a **dog** have this kind of **relationship** before. They have a

# Strange Love!!!

## Strange Love!!!

Love knows no boundaries, as is evident in the unusual relationship between Kim's cat and dog. This loving duo snuggles up on Kim's layout, which uses a large journaling block incorporating a prominent title to balance out the photo. To accentuate key words that define this politically incorrect couple, Kim peppered the passage with slightly larger bold fonts. Sheer silky ribbon borders elicit a romantic touch, complementing the cozy pink papers. A stylish row of silver brads, embellished by a large photo brad and love sticker, repeat the look of the collar from the photo with amorous attitude.

Kim Musgrove, Lewiston, New York

**Supplies:** Patterned papers (K & Company); textured cardstock (Bazzill); ribbon (Offray); photo brad, love sticker (Pebbles); crystal lacquer (Sakura Hobby Craft); brads

## A Day in the Life of a Diva

It's a dog's life, and Kylie the springer spaniel loves it, as is evident on this energetic page. According to Kathy, Kylie is constantly in motion, so she added swirl punches to the tops of each tag to convey this sense of perpetual movement. Each colorful cardstock tag features an image of Kylie in action and progresses through this much-loved pooch's day. Kathy created her own stencil letter with cardstock and patterned paper and embellished it with ribbon and bows. She added her own stripes to black wooden letters to coordinate with the striped paper and to add further excitement to the page.

Kathy Montgomery, Rocklin, California

**Supplies:** Patterned papers (American Crafts, My Mind's Eye); textured cardstocks (Bazzill); rub-on letters (Wordsworth); letter stickers (Me & My Big Ideas, Wordsworth); ribbons (Offray), wooden letters (Wal-Mart); mini brads (Making Memories); distress ink (Ranger); flower punch (EK Success); transparency; cardstock; acrylic paint

## So Busted

Shuri's Jack Russell terrier, Popcorn, obeyed the "stay!" command just long enough after emerging from the cupboard to retrieve her favorite treat for Shuri to snap this incriminating photo. She designed her layout around the colors of the contraband, using large jigsaw letters to perfectly describe the moment. Letter stickers were used to form a label across two cardstock tags, creating the look of dog tags beneath Popcorn's "mug shot." Fancy fibers lend a touch of feminine fun to Shuri's journaling tag, pocketed on the left.

Shuri Orr, Dawsonville, Georgia

**Supplies:** Patterned papers, letter stickers (Basic Grey); flower, mini brads, chipboard letters (Making Memories); letter brads (Colorbök); fibers; stamping ink

## Cat and Mouse

A modern-day game of cat-and-mouse is the main event on Jennie's comedic layout featuring the zany antics of her attention-starved kitten. Jennie used photo-editing software to alter the image so that the computer mouse would be the main focus. An assortment of letter stickers were used to create the title while charming green buttons add a touch of dimension and help pull a vibrant hue from the patterned paper.

Jennie Freeman, Boise, Idaho

**Supplies:** Patterned paper (Karen Foster Design); textured cardstock (Bazzill); image-editing software (Adobe Photoshop Elements); letter stickers (Provo Craft); date stamp (Making Memories); buttons (Wal-Mart); rub-on letters (KI Memories); stamping ink; transparency

## Whack

A swift swipe to the forehead from Britton's dog, Dozer, creates a great action shot on Amy's layout featuring the playful pair. Amy used software to design the boys-will-be-boys feel of this page, arranging custom shapes found in the program. The disclaimer at the bottom of the layout, along with the action word set in a whimsical font, add humorous touches and a reassurance that this scene is a non-threatening part of everyday life with Dozer.

Amy Johansson, Mesa, Arizona

**Supplies:** Image-editing software (Adobe Photoshop)

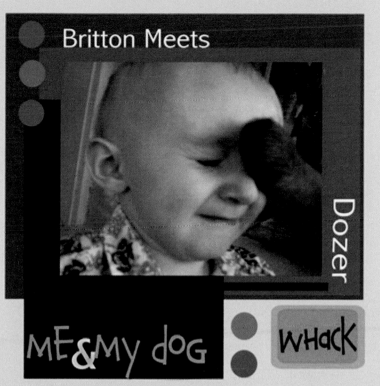

Britton Meets Dozer

ME&My doG : WHacK

**no child or dog was harmed in the making of this layout**

Michaela and Casey the Kitty have a very unique relationship. Even though Michaela terrorizes Casey, jumps at her, screams at her in delight -- Casey still has the love to share a lick and a kiss whenever she can.

Kitty Kisses

## Kitty Kisses

Unconditional love is at its best in this photo depicting Michaela, who loves to terrorize and torment Casey the Kitty, being kindly licked and loved on by her nonetheless. Doris kept her computer-generated design clean and simple to keep the focus on the tenderness displayed in the photo. All papers, fibers and embellishments were downloaded from the Internet and creatively arranged to form this adorable page.

Doris Castle, Fonda, New York

**Supplies:** Patterned papers (Love List Page Pak, www.cottagearts.net); heart charm (Valentine Page Pak, www.cottagearts.net); flower charm (Retro Page Pak, www.cottagearts.net); brushed heart, fiber (www.cottagearts.net)

A beautiful spring day

+ a curious puppy

+ me watering the trees

# ONE WET DOG

Today was a beautiful, April day. For the first time in a week, it wasn't windy and spring was definitely in the air. Jordan got the idea to clean up the backyard a bit, so the four of us (Jord, me, Gizmo, and Max) went outside. I watered the trees and bushes while Jordan trimmed all the dead brush and cleaned things up.

Watching Max today, I was totally reminded of how much fun it is to have a puppy. This is Max's first spring, and everything is new to him. He was absolutely adorable. He had to have his nose in everything, and kept trying to drink the water as it came out of the sprayer. Within minutes he was soaked, and found that it was a lot of fun to run his wet body back and forth underneath the wet bushes and roll in the muddy gravel.

Gizmo, being 5 years old and much more mature spent most of the time on the deck watching the puppy run back and forth across the backyard. After I turned off the sprayer he did come down to have some playtime with Max; and I could not stop laughing at them. They're so funny when they play because they are the best of friends. We love these two dogs, and they sure makes things a lot more interesting around here.

## One Wet Dog

Jenna re-created a beautiful April day spent outside with her new puppy on this vibrant two-page spread. On the left, she sanded the edges of the focal-point photo and stamped a paw print border around it to reflect her pup's muddy feet. She highlighted the word "wet" by painting the back of each foam stamp letter, stamping a square, and then adding the stamped letters inside once the squares were dry. The right page showcases Jenna's puppy at play and includes a small collage in the upper right corner.

**Jenna Slomp, Lethbridge, Alberta, Canada**

**Supplies:** Patterned paper (KI Memories); textured cardstock (Bazzill); foam letter stamps; metal signage (Making Memories); metal paw print plate (American Traditional Designs); paw print stamp (Stampendous!); rub-on numbers (Li'l Davis Designs); ribbon; stamping ink; staples

A **dog's tendency to roll in the grass** is **linked to its wolf ancestry**, in which "rolling" in a scent was done to bring the scent back to the rest of the pack.

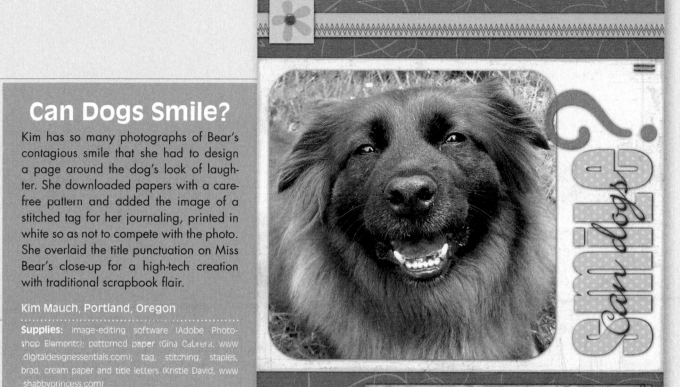

## Can Dogs Smile?

Kim has so many photographs of Bear's contagious smile that she had to design a page around the dog's look of laughter. She downloaded papers with a carefree pattern and added the image of a stitched tag for her journaling, printed in white so as not to compete with the photo. She overlaid the title punctuation on Miss Bear's close-up for a high-tech creation with traditional scrapbook flair.

Kim Mauch, Portland, Oregon

**Supplies:** Image-editing software (Adobe Photoshop Elements); patterned paper (Gina Cabrera, www.digitaldesignessentials.com); tag, stitching, staples, brad, cream paper and title letters (Kristie David, www.shabbyprincess.com)

# Tips for Working With Pet-Themed Products

Pet-themed scrapbook products are just the ticket for putting your pet pages over the top, but can be tricky to use for their bold prints and patterns. Consider the following tips while working with these whimsical papers and page additions.

- Use only portions of bold patterned papers in the form of blocks, bars or photo mats.
- Combine small segments of coordinating papers from the same line as opposed to large sections or entire backgrounds.
- Cut select words, phrases and images from patterned papers to use as titles and accents.
- Ink or sand the edges of punch-outs and die cuts and mount them on foam adhesive.
- Incorporate neutral papers and cardstocks to tone down vibrant colors and patterns.
- Downplay overpowering backgrounds with a vellum overlay, or alter with light distressing or colorants.
- Combine papers and accents from other lines.
- Mix the scale, or size, of patterned paper prints for eye-pleasing balance.
- Ink or stitch the edges of overlapping patterns for to make each paper "pop."
- Be selective with themed page accents for just-the-right finishing touches.

## Le Chat Ali

The sunny background from the popular Steinlen Art Nouveau poster inspired this layout dedicated to Ali the cat's sunbathing addiction. To re-create the look of the Steinlen piece, Nicole scanned the sticker replica at the bottom of her page, enlarged it to create the large black cat, and then cut out the image from black paper. Each poster sticker was mounted on cardstock and embellished with ribbons and decorative brads to complete the look.

Nicole Keller, Rio Hondo, Texas

Supplies: Patterned paper, stickers (Provo Craft); ribbons (Making Memories, Michaels, Offray); fleur-de-lis brads (Creative Expressions); square brads (Making Memories); pen; marker; cardstock

## A Lab's Best Friend

It's the simple things in life that bring the most joy for Lori's Labrador retriever, Drake, so she designed this page to express his passion for stick fetching. Lori kept the page simple and rustic by using earthy tones and jute accents. Torn paper edges and frayed jute ends capture the rough-and-tumble attitude of her playful pooch. She created the multimedia effect of her title by simply cutting out elements from patterned papers.

Lori Bokavich, Shasta, California

Supplies: Patterned papers (7 Gypsies, Chatterbox, EK Success, Hot Off The Press); date stamp (Office Max); square eyelets (Making Memories); cardstock; staples; jute; stamping ink

## Dream

Margie's cat, Nadia, is such a character in their family that she created this layout as a tribute to all her funny feline traits. Margie printed the image of Nadia's catnap on fabric to evoke a peaceful, dreamlike quality, which she further softened with stitched detail. She then tucked three colorful tags accented with textural ribbons behind the cat-themed paper at the bottom of the page. Each tag pulls out to reveal journaling on the back describing memorable antics and characteristics of this feline extraordinaire.

**Margie Oliveira, Fall River, Massachusetts**

**Supplies:** Patterned papers (Flair Designs, Junkitz); textured cardstock (Bazzill); ribbon, cardstock stickers, metal charm (Flair Designs); inkjet printer fabric (June Tailor); letter stickers (Wordsworth); fabric

## Goofy

Laura used bright colors and energetic patterns to create a playful feel on this comical page featuring her dog Rocky. She loved the look of Rocky with his tongue hanging haphazardly out of his mouth and wanted a page design filled with energy and playfulness. Laura threaded ribbons through a large letter monogram for texture and embossed with watermark ink for dimensional shine.

**Laura McKinley, Westport, Connecticut**

**Supplies:** Patterned papers (Basic Grey); textured cardstock (Bazzill); monogram letter (My Mind's Eye); rubber stamps (Technique Tuesday); watermark ink (Tsukineko); rub on letters (Li'l Davis Designs); transparency (Magic Scraps); ribbon (May Arts); stamping ink; acrylic paint; pen

## Waiting on the Mail

Where there's a will there's a way for Marlene's oversized cat, who creatively made his way atop the mailbox to take a snooze. Marlene snapped the top right photo from inside the house, then went outside for a closer look. Horizontal patterns, ribbons and bands of color reflect the stretched-out image of this furry sleeping beauty, as well as the lines from the window in the focal photo. A metal-rimmed tag and a playful pet charm accented with ribbon enhance the page theme.

Marlene Clawser, Pinellas Park, Florida

Supplies: Patterned paper (Autumn Leaves); textured cardstock (WorldWin); ribbons (May Arts); letter stickers (Deja Views); rub-on letters (Autumn Leaves, Li'l Davis Designs); metal fish charm (Flair Designs); metal-rimmed tag (Making Memories); eyelet ball chain (Pebbles); brads

Waiting ON the MAIL

Our cat picks some silly spots to lay, this being one of them. I looked out the front window one day and found him spread out on the mailbox. I took this picture from inside the house and then I had to go outside to get a better view. As you can see, he is not a small cat so I have no idea how he managed to get himself up on the mailbox without sliding off. He just sort of sprawled across the top of it. Doesn't seem like it would be all that comfortable but he liked it enough that he was out there sunning himself quite a few times. And he didn't even jump down when our postman came by. I actually stood inside and watched the mailman lift up Mono's paw, open the mailbox, put the mail inside and then put his paw back down. Mono hardly opened his eyes. He just loves people and especially when they make a fuss over him so it didn't surprise me that he just stayed there sleeping. He actually belongs to our son but when he moved he couldn't take him right away so we said he could stay here, that was over 4 years ago so I think that means we've offically adopted him. I wasn't really a "cat" person before he came to live with us but I have come to love him so much that it would seem lonely if he weren't around to entertain us with his silly ways.

Life According to Elijah
- Always find a good patch of sun to nap in.
- Nap often.
- When in trouble, just purr and look cute.
- Life is hard, and then you nap.
- In a cat's eye, all things belong to cats.
- As every cat owner knows, nobody owns a cat.
- When in doubt, nap.

## Home Is Where the Cat Is

As Elijah so aptly demonstrates, it doesn't get much better than catnaps. The luxurious velvet ribbons tie in beautifully with Elijah's fur and further the posh look of his fluffy bedding. A metal expression charm tied to the center of the ribbon personalizes this sleepy cat's page with pet-themed pizazz and adds further dimension as well. Melanie's journaling shares wisdom from her cat, printed in a bulleted format onto cardstock.

Melanie Douthit, West Monroe, Louisiana
Photo: Staci C. Ojeda, Melissa, Texas

Supplies: Patterned paper, velvet ribbon, tag, metal charm (Flair Designs); textured cardstock (Bazzill); ribbon (Jcaroline Creative!); chalk ink (Clearsnap); acrylic paint

When a **cat** holds its **tail high**, it is **happy**. When a cat **twitches** its tail, it is **a warning sign.**

**TOBY**

A Day In The Life Of A

Pampered Pooch

Toby at 10

| 4:55 AM: | Dad's alarm goes off in 5 minutes, but since I'm awake I think I'll just go to the door and start barking. I really need to go outside, what's 5 minutes anyway? |
| 5:00 AM: | I think Dad might be mad at me. He sure didn't seem to happy 5 minutes ago. |
| 5:05 AM: | Hmmm, it was a little cold out there this morning. Time to go cuddle up by Mom. I can get a couple more hours of sleep before she gets up for the day. |
| 7:12 AM: | Ok, I sure hope she doesn't hit that snooze alarm again. Time for me to get this household up and at 'em for the day. Off to the door for a little bit o' barking. |
| 7:20 AM: | Now that they're all up, time for me to take my mid-morning nap. Under Mom & Dad's bed, here I come. |
| 7:48 AM: | The family is out the door and on their way for the day. Finally, some peace and quiet. I've got to get rested up for tonight when we're all home together again. |
| 11:00 AM: | Sleep |
| 2:00 PM: | More sleep |
| 4:05 PM: | Mom's home! Mom's home! Bark, bark, bark, time for me to go explore the backyard. |
| 4:15 PM: | Dad's home! Dad's home! Time for my afternoon walk! It's my favorite time of day. |
| 4:30 PM: | There's my food bowl. I'm a little thirsty after my walk. The water isn't quite as cold as I like, if I whine long enough I know someone will give me a cold drink. |
| 4:45 PM: | Time for my late afternoon nap. I'll just lay on my blanket in the living room. That way I won't miss anything. |
| 5:30 PM: | Mom says it's time to get one of the kids from practice. Time for me to go bye-bye in the car. Yippy! |
| 7:00 PM: | Supper time! Bark, bark, whine, whine.... someone please fill my bowl. |
| 8:00 PM: | Time for an evening nap. Sure hope Mom wants to read so I can sit in her lap. |
| 9:30 PM: | Bed time. C'mon Dad. Five o'clock comes pretty early in the morning |

## A Day in the Life of a Pampered Pooch

Because her pampered pooch is such a character, Peggy decided that for a fun approach to her page, she'd document a day in his life from his perspective. Since barking is one of Toby's favorite pastimes, she highlighted the word "bark" with a coordinating blue chalk each time it appeared in her journaling. Although the camera caught a glare in Toby's eyes, Peggy did a great job working her page around the blue circles, utilizing patterned papers with the same shade of blue, as well as circle patterns in both papers and ribbons. She even included rhinestone brads for extra shimmer and shine.

Peggy Nardini, Madrid, Iowa

**Supplies:** Patterned papers, ribbon, circle tag, letter stickers, rhinestone brads (SEI); textured cardstock (Bazzill); die-cut letters (QuickKutz); transparency; stamping ink; chalk; pen

## The Rose

When Kathi's cat, Flash, swiped a silk rose from a vase, Kathi knew she had to create a page to commemorate this new favorite yet highly unorthodox toy. She loved the rose hue found in these patterned papers and layered the lively designs beneath the photos and journaling, while she set the coordinating monograms against a more solid, distressed look for contrast. Kathi took apart two different sizes of silk flowers, assembled them into one, and then ironed and inked the petals to form the thematic element at the bottom of the page.

Kathi Rerek, Scotch Plains, New Jersey

**Supplies:** Patterned papers, monogram letters (Basic Grey); die-cut letters (QuicKutz); thumbtack brad (Karen Foster Design); distress ink (Ranger); silk flowers

Cats, like children, choose some odd toys. Flash proved this to be true when he pulled a pink plastic rose out of a vase and ran away with it. He carried it throughout the house in his mouth, slept with it, and would growl if Duchess or one of us came near it. It was one of his favorite toys 'til it fell apart.

If I like it, it's mine.
If it's in my mouth, it's mine
If I can take it from you, it's mine.
If it's mine, it must never appear to be yours in any way.
If I'm chewing something up, all the pieces are mine
If it just looks like mine, it's mine.
If I saw it first, it's mine.
If you are playing with something and you put it down, it automatically becomes mine.
If it's broken, it's yours.

## Dog Property Laws

Carmel had always wanted to illustrate a humorous poem with one of her photos, and this image of her dog was the perfect muse to bring about this page describing the property laws of dogs. Bright colors and lighthearted patterns evoke a playful mood on Carmel's page and whimsically emphasize the dog toy theme. Cut patterned paper circles adorned with spiral clips reinforce the energetic pattern at the top of the page.

Carmel Flores, Westfield, Indiana

**Supplies:** Patterned papers (KI Memories); spiral clips (Warmcuddles Embellishments)

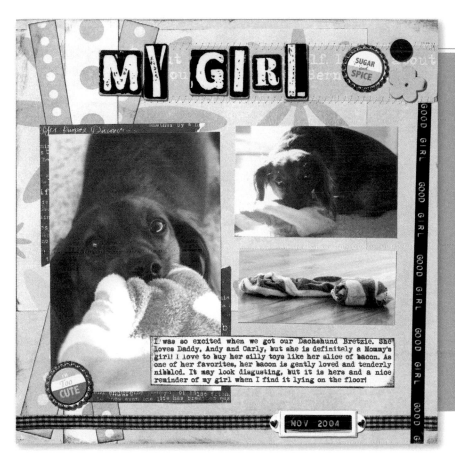

## My Girl

Although dogs are more than willing to spread their love, the fact remains that it is their primal nature to save a soft spot for whom they determine to be the "Alpha" dog of their pack. In this endearing layout, Tricia reveals it is she who holds this coveted spot in Bretzie's heart. So to spoil her little sweetheart, Tricia loves to shower her with spceial dog toys like the "bacon" toy featured. Feminine pink patterned papers and accents play up this girly girl page while black accents and ink smudged edges provide eye-appealing contrast.

**Tricia Rubens, Castle Rock, Colorado**

**Supplies:** Patterned papers (7 Gypsies, Imagination Project); bottle caps, bottle cap stickers (Design Originals); label maker (Dymo); ribbon (May Arts); buttons, label holder, leather flower (Making Memories); stamping ink

## Caught in the Act

There's no denying Heather's ornery puppy is guilty as charged, with evidence as indisputable as these photos! As Heather snapped these shots of Gracie having her way with a can of Jif, this choosy pup never once even batted an eye. This layout uses brilliant colors for a lighthearted look at Gracie's antics and colorful letter stickers with pet-themed flair to comple ment the peanut butter label. Buttons and ribbons add pizazz to the page, topped off by a sleek paw print charm.

**Heather Preckel,
Swannanoa, North Carolina**

**Supplies:** Patterned paper, letter stickers, paw print charms (American Traditional Designs); textured cardstock (Bazzill); ribbon (Michaels); buttons (Junkitz); foam adhesive spacers

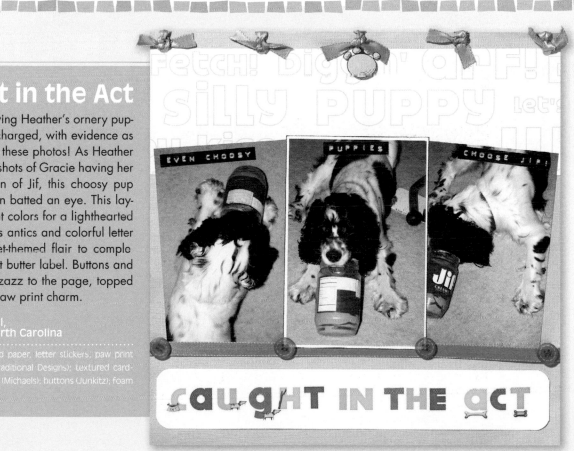

A **cat** will spend nearly **30% of his life grooming** himself.

# Packet Time

The internal clock of a hungry cat is not a force to be taken lightly, a fact Melanie chronicles in this page describing her cat's persistent pursuit for food packets at the same time each day. Melanie used an oversized photo of her cat, Thomas, to fill up the bulk of the page, adding rub-on title letters directly onto the print. She layered strips of clock-themed paper and decorative vellum on the left and used a concho and colorful brads to accentuate the circular pattern. Along the right side, Melanie describes Thomas' determined demeanor when it comes to getting his grub.

**Melanie Bauer, Columbia, Missouri**

**Supplies:** Patterned paper (Rusty Pickle); textured cardstock (Bazzill); decorative vellum (American Crafts); concho (Scrapworks); mini brads (Boxer Scrapbook Productions); rub-on letters (Making Memories); rub-on date (Autumn Leaves); pen

packet time. the time in the afternoon when thomas decides that he must have his packet of wet food — around 4pm during the week and as early as 1pm on the weekend. and if he doesn't get his food when he wants it — beware! soon, the meowing will begin. face it, trying to stick to a schedule just isn't worth it. thomas and his internal clock are not to be reckoned with!

## Patriotic Puppy

Thrilled to have found a new home with Katie's family, Mocha, free at last, parades around the yard waving her flag in sheer jubilation. Katie downloaded Americana-themed papers to complement the passion of her patriotic pup and added a chipboard letter round to polish off this digital delight. By angling the filmstrip frame over the accent photo, Katie enhances the realism of her design to appear as more of a traditional scrapbook page.

**Katie Pertiet, Naperville, Illinois**

**Supplies:** Patterned papers (Americana Paper Pack, www.designerdigitals.com); chipboard letter, film negative frame (www.designerdigitals.com)

PATRIOTIC *puppy*

THIS WAS MOCHA'S FIRST DAY WITH OUR FAMILY AND SHE WAS HAPPY TO PERFORM SOME TRICKS SO WE KNEW WE GOT QUITE THE SPECIAL PUPPY!

MAY 26, 2003

WHERE'S *grady?*

## Where's Grady?

The closest way to capture Grady's personality in a photo was to find him in his element—the pantry—and to showcase his treasure trove on the page. In this collection of items found on Grady's pantry shelf, Colette used solid colors and clean lines in her page design so as to not compete with the photos. She used rub-on numbers over each pantry item in the left photo and included corresponding numbered tags describing each goody below. An image of Grady's favorite treat is elevated in the top center with foam adhesive spacers for dimension.

**Colette Bate, Gilbert, Arizona**

**Supplies:** Textured cardstock (Bazzill); ribbons (Offray); rub-on letters and numbers (Making Memories)

# Wanna Play?

Who could resist such a sweet face begging for a few moments of play? Yolanda used playful patterns and sunny colors to capture Scooter's carefree attitude and created accents with brown ribbons to complement the Frisbee champ's fur. A label sticker applied at an angle across the the page creates a strong dynamic and ties in with the ribbons set across the left corners. Torn paper edges lend visual fun and the look of puppy play to this cheerful design.

Yolanda Williams,
Charlotte, North Carolina

**Supplies:** Patterned paper (Paper Reflections); textured cardstock (Bazzill); ribbons (Morex Corp.); letter stickers, brads (Making Memories); photo turns (7 Gypsies); label maker (Dymo)

The day was Tuesday, 04-19-05 at approx. 6:30 PM. We finished our dinner and we let him out for his normal bathroom run.

Well, Scooter comes back with his "outside toy" - the FRISBEE!!!

Scooter looked so pitiful that I just excused myself from our company long enough to snag the camera and take a few shots; because he was so doggone cute standing there with that frisbee hanging out of his mouth! Scooter obviously knows camera moments because he poses - I kid you not, he POSES!!!

Once our quick shoot was over we played his favorite game of Frisbee until he got tired (30 minutes).

I just love my Scooter!

---

Don't be fooled by the sweet face...there's enough spunk behind those yellow eyes to get into a world of mischief!

Despite her daily antics that keep us on our toes, Roxy is adored by all. Lift the "O" to read about her exploits.

# Roxy

Tamara's cat, Roxy, has enough mischief behind those big yellow eyes to fill a small book. In fact, Tamara created a small booklet detailing Roxy's daily antics and cleverly concealed it behind the large flower "o" element in her title. She began by printing Roxy's rambunctious behaviors, which she then cut into circles and bound with a coordinating brad. For the journaling beneath the photo, Tamara printed directly onto patterned paper with a large format printer by setting her margins to line up exactly along the solid stripes.

Tamara Morrison,
Trabuco Canyon, California

**Supplies:** Patterned papers, die-cut letters (FontWerks); textured cardstock (Bazzill); brad (Making Memories)

10 reasons why **Keisha** thinks she's human

1. She comes when she's called.
2. She answers when I call her name.
3. She drinks out of a running faucet.
4. Her favorite positions are in my lap or over my shoulder.
5. She loves cantaloupe and cottage cheese.
6. She can hold a conversation with me (in Kitty Speak).
7. She knows the word treat.
8. She lies down with my children until they fall asleep.
9. She sleeps in my bed.
10. She sleeps with her head on the pillow UNDER the covers.

purr · cat nip · mouser · kitty · feline · frisky · paws · nine lives · cat nap · play · yarn · frisky · mouser · whiskers · meow · best friend · spoiled

## 10 Reasons Why Keisha Thinks She's Human

JoAnne's pet, Keisha, may be a cat, but she believes in her heart she is a human. JoAnne created this page to share the crazy people tricks her cat performs, from sleeping under the covers with her head on a pillow, to eating cantaloupe with cottage cheese! The pet-themed twill tape led JoAnne to create this simple layout featuring a single photo, a touch of ribbon and journaling printed directly on the cardstock background.

**JoAnne Bacon, Alpharetta, Georgia**

**Supplies:** Patterned paper (SEI); printed twill (Carolee's Creations); paw print stamp (Stampin' Up!)

## Happy Hour

It's an open bar for Max and Gus! These two thirsty dogs aren't picky about the source of their beverages, and Lisa found after seeing this photo that she just had to build a layout around it. She formed her large title letter by tracing a purchased monogram onto sheet metal, adhering it over a cardstock replica and mounting it on foam adhesive spacers. The dark color scheme and distressed look of the papers lend a masculine look to the page, with the flair of a pub, strengthened in humor with the paw print ribbon.

**Lisa Nielsen, Elk Point, Alberta, Canada**

**Supplies:** Patterned paper (Basic Grey); ribbon, screw top brads (Scraptivity); rub-on letters (Making Memories); die-cut letters (Sizzix); metal sheet (AMACO); cardstock; acrylic paint; foam adhesive spacers

happy hour — WheN the LiDs UP— drinks aRe FrEe

## Sun Spot

Looking on the sunny side of things is all part of Melanie's cat Thomas' daily routine, so she created this warm layout to commemorate his affinity for snoozing in, and soaking up, the rays. Melanie added file tabs to the right side of the page to spell out her sun-worshiper's name and set a yellow concho on top of the title block for thematic effect.

**Melanie Bauer, Columbia, Missouri**

**Supplies:** Patterned papers (KI Memories, Scenic Route Paper Co.); textured cardstock (Bazzill); foam letter stamps (Making Memories); concho (Scrapworks); tabs (Autumn Leaves); acrylic paint; stamping ink

## Gecko Green

As Summer set out to scrap a layout one day, she was surprised beyond words to find a gecko making a home in her stack of green cardstock! She created this page to remember the now-hilarious memory, using ribbons and machine-stitching to tie in with the scrapbook workstation locale. Summer scanned her color wheel, enlarged it and trimmed out the openings to frame her little green friend in his familiar color.

**Summer Ford, Bulverde, Texas**

**Supplies:** Textured cardstock (Bazzill); color wheel (EK Success); foam letter stamps, eyelet (Making Memories); ribbon (Offray); hole punch (Fiskars); eyelet; date stamp; sewing machine

Many species of **geckos** possess specialized **toe pads** that enable them to **easily scale smooth vertical surfaces and ceilings.**

## The Grass Is Always Greener

When Christina discovered that her dog, Kai, was sneaking into the neighbor's yard and swiping their dog's toys, she knew she had to capture every step of Kai's deviant behavior on film. Photo-editing software was used to resize and crop each mischievous image into the squares set along the bottom of the design. Painted corrugated paper set behind the large letter stencil creates an outdoorsy ruggedness on the page, as well as a powerful title embellishment. Mesh behind the photos on the upper right mimic the look and feel of Kai's fence.

Christina Buckley, Mahina Bay, Wellington, New Zealand

**Supplies:** Patterned paper (Paper Loft); textured cardstock (Bazzill); bamboo clip (7 Gypsies); mesh (Creative Imaginations); letter stamps (Hero Arts); image-editing software (Adobe Photoshop Elements 2.0); eyelets (Happy Hammer); stencil letter (ChartPak); word buttons (Jesse James); stamping ink; acrylic paint

A **dog's sense of smell** is about 1,000 times stronger than a human's and their **hearing** is sensitive to sounds inaudible to people, such as very high pitches. A dog's **eyesight**, however, is weaker than a human's.

My dog is an extraordinary person.

# An Interview With a Dog

Laura knows her dog so well she can nearly read his thoughts, as she demonstrates in this nonverbal interview conducted for Thunder's layout. No longer having to wonder what the exhausted pup is thinking, Laura shares Thunder's likes, dislikes and how he wishes his diet would change. Laura kept the left page simple, using a single portrait of Thunder balanced by a more-than-true framed stamp element. The right is reserved for the interview and several photos of Thunder's favorite creature comforts.

**Laura Stewart, Fort Wayne, Indiana**

**Supplies:** Patterned paper, cardstock stickers (SEI); textured cardstock (Bazzill); mini brads, paper piercer (Lasting Impressions); letter stamps (Hero Arts); stamp (Catslife Press); circle punch (EK Success)

## an interview with a dog

On the day of our meeting, Thunder was looking exceptionally tired. I wondered what could be bothering him on this surprisingly sunny winter morning.

When we began the interview Thunder seemed nervous, pacing back and forth between the chair and the French doors. It was as though he was waiting for someone to arrive.

As an icebreaker, I asked Thunder what he liked best about being a dog. Although there was no verbal reply to this question, he did answer with his eyes. He said the thing he loves most about being a dog is having such a loving family to call his own. Not everyone has that.

Thunder went on to respond to questions about his likes and dislikes, the doggie dating scene, and how he manages to stay in such great physical shape.

Thunder showed his favorite piece of his wardrobe, his new suede and fur jacket, and he illustrated that he never goes anywhere without his black leather collar that he received for his birthday a few years back. He has a lot of Personal Style.

Thunder seemed much more relaxed as the interview proceeded, and I introduced some questions about his puppyhood memories. I asked him if he was close to his parents, and he indicated that he was separated from them shortly after birth.

I noticed a scar on his tongue but resisted the urge to ask him where it came from. It appeared to be left behind by some sort of injury.

If he could change anything – anything at all – Thunder wishes that he could enjoy some of the rich tasting foods that his family brings home. Unfortunately Thunder suffers from a sensitive stomach, so he's on a strict diet of Lamb and Rice.

I finally decided to call our meeting quits when Thunder nodded off. He was clearly exhausted. It *is* pretty hard being a dog.

Love ya

## Got Busted

Busted while relaxing on the good chair, Jake earned himself this humorous page which sets the date in stone. Liana stamped and embossed paw prints across the layout and onto the photo, incorporating her dog's mischievous behavior into the scene of the crime. She traced a letter stencil onto patterned paper and then inked the edges of the paper beneath to coordinate with the white paper. Staples and tied closures give an official "permanent record" feel to the page and add dimension as well.

Liana Suwandi, Wylie, Texas

Photo: Frendy Moesa, Wylie, Texas

Supplies: Patterned papers (DieCuts with a View, Mustard Moon); textured cardstock (Bazzill); letter stencil (Office Max); sticker (Pebbles); letter stamps (source unknown); paw print stamp (Stampendous!); stamping ink; embossing powder; staples; paper reinforcements; eyelets; thread; foam adhesive spacers

## Journaling Prompts

- How you knew your pet was **special**
- The story behind your pet's **name**
- Things **you have learned** from your pet
- Your pet's **facts** and stats
- Interesting information about your **pet's species**
- **Silliest habits, quirks** and characteristics of your pet
- Top **reasons you love** your pet
- **Favorite memory** with your pet
- Your pet's **favorite food**, treats, toys, etc.
- Your pet's typical **daily routine**
- **Naughtiest thing** your pet has ever done
- Life **according to** your pet
- Conduct an **"interview"** with your pet
- Write a letter from your **pet's perspective**

COKI

THE WATER D

Yes, this is our pet. No dogs, no cats...a Chinese Water Dragon...named Co-ki! His diet? Living crickets, meal worms...anything disgusting! Ha-ha! But for as aggressive as water dragons look to some, he is the most gentle and funny animal we've had since our ferret! (ah-ki!) Yes, this house is not your average pet loving home. Just a Guinea pig, ferret and Chinese Water Dragon for the Stamtoles household!! ☺ Pssst....Co-ki even has a leash! ~2004~

# chapter three | Pet Personalities

They're lovable, lazy, sweet and saucy—perhaps a tad neurotic at times. Yet the more we come to learn who our pets are at their core, the more we realize that, much like little people, they come complete with their own inherent spirits and personalities. As you create scrapbook pages that celebrate your pet, be sure to capture their wild-at-heart attitudes, wrinkles of disdain, mischievous sparks and prima donna prissiness. What can't be reigned into a photo can certainly be expressed through your journaling, so preserve each paw print your pet makes on your heart with pages that define the soul behind each bundle of fur, feathers or fins.

## Shy Boy

Cotter the cat has such a soft disposition, Kristen had to create a layout to showcase his sweet personality and quiet strength. She took these natural-light photos in a sunny room during morning hours and brought the camera down to Cotter's level for close-ups. Gold brads and eyelets highlight this shy cat's eyes, while the deep plum background and orange patterned papers and accents draw out the colors from his tiger-striped fur.

**Liana Suwandi, Wylie, Texas**
**Photo: Frendy Moesa, Wylie, Texas**

**Supplies:** Patterned papers (Flair Designs); letter stickers (Sticker Studio); pet-themed stickers (Boxer Scrapbook Productions, Flair Designs); ribbon (Offray); photo corners (Canson); eyelets; brads

## Ma Lumiere...

Isabelle's cat, Capucine, provides perpetual joy and loving company, which inspired her to design this warm page around her cat being such a ray of sunshine. The orange patterned papers complement the look of the sun on her cat's fur and expand upon the page theme. She used a craft knife to handcut her title letters and created the look of illumination on the page by dabbing the borders with dark brown ink.

**Isabelle L'Italien, Montreal, Quebec, Canada**

**Supplies:** Patterned Paper (Imagination Project); textured cardstock (Bazzill); brads; stamping ink

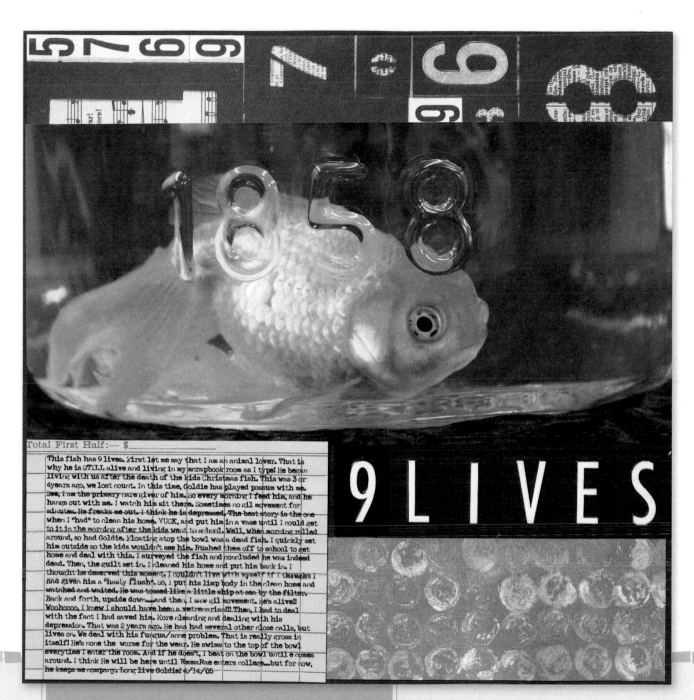

9LIVES

Total First Half:— $

This fish has 9 lives. First let me say that I am an animal lover. That is why he is STILL alive and living in my scrapbook room as I type! He began living with us after the death of the kids Christmas fish. This was 3 or 4years ago, we lost count. In this time, Goldie has played possum with me. See, I am the primary care giver of him. So every morning I feed him, and he hangs out with me. I watch him sit there. Sometimes no gil movement for minutes. He freaks me out. I think he is depressed. The best story is the one when I "had" to clean his home. YUCK, and put him in a vase until I could get to it in the morning after the kids went to school. Well, when morning rolled around, so had Goldie. Floating atop the bowl was a dead fish. I quickly set him outside so the kids wouldn't see him. Rushed them off to school to get home and deal with this. I surveyed the fish and concluded he was indeed dead. Then, the guilt set in. I cleaned his home and put him back in. I thought he deserved this moment. I couldn't live with myself if I thought I had given him a "hasty flush". So, I put his limp body in the clean home and watched and waited. He was tossed like a little ship at sea by the filter. Back and forth, upside down...and then, I saw gil movement. He's alive!! Woohoooo, I knew I should have been a vetrenarian!!! Then, I had to deal with the fact I had saved him. More cleaning and dealing with his depression. That was 2 years ago. He has had several other close calls, but lives on. We deal with his fungus/acne problem. That is really gross in itself! He's none the worse for the wear. He swims to the top of the bowl everytime I enter the room. And if he doest, I beat on the bowl until e comes around. I think He will be here until EmmaRae enters collage...but for now, he keeps me company. Long live Goldie! 4/14/05

## 9 Lives

Goldie, the eternal fish, found a home in Judith's scrapbook as a way to remember the numerous times he has "played possum" and been found floating at the top of his bowl, the prankster that he is! Judith cropped an 8 x 12" image of Goldie to create a dynamic effect against the mailbox letters and patterned papers that mimic the numbers on his bowl and the appearance of his scales. Judith printed her journaling onto a transparency and adhered it to patterned paper for visual interest.

Judith Fender, Fletcher, North Carolina

**Supplies:** Patterned papers (EK Success, Li'l Davis Designs, Rusty Pickle); letter stickers (Making Memories); cardstock; transparency

Goldfish are the most popular household pets in the world, and the most popular name given to goldfish today is "Jaws."

## Pretty as a Peach

Since Michelle is often busy designing masculine pages of her little boy, she loves to create ultra-girly pages in honor of her pretty-as-a-peach pug. Here Michelle ran with the hint of Peach's pink tongue to create a fun, frilly and festive design. She curved her title word around a large, cut-out circle inked with brown for cohesiveness and repeated the bouncy pattern with chipboard letter circles. Epoxy stickers add sassy shimmer to the layout, while the ribbon band and buckle beneath the photo create the illusion of a sleek dog collar.

Michelle Hubbartt, Grand Junction, Colorado

**Supplies:** Patterned papers (Imagination Project, Making Memories); personal media cutter (Wishblade); textured cardstock (Bazzill); ribbons (May Arts, Offray); chipboard circles, rub-on letters (Heidi Swapp); ribbon buckle (Making Memories); epoxy stickers (Creative Imaginations); stamping ink

## Belle

Layers of pink paisleys and dancing flowers bring out the best of Belle on Amanda's layout. She created this page to showcase the feminine personality of her beautiful feline and to explain through journaling the story behind this diva-kitty's name. Amanda added pink paint to enhance the metal heart charm and printed the meaning of Belle's name on a transparency found in the lower left.

Amanda Palmer, Billerica, Massachusetts

**Supplies:** Patterned paper (Chatterbox); chipboard letters, metal accent (Making Memories); acrylic paint; cardstock

**Cats purr** at the **same frequency** as an **idling diesel engine**: about **26 cycles per second**.

## The Face of a Killer?

Sweet innocence overflows from this beloved Rottweiler's face onto the endearing design created on her behalf. Emily grew discouraged one summer when she learned her dog Hannah's breed was banned from a campground where she and her family wanted to vacation. Emily used soft colors and patterns suited to her gentle dog's personality and contrasted the effect with license plate letter stickers that express the stigma associated with the breed.

Emily Burrough, San Diego, California

**Supplies:** Patterned papers (Chatterbox, EK Success); letter stickers (Sticker Studio); index tab (Creek Bank Creations); brad (Making Memories); corner rounder (Marvy); distress ink (Ranger); rickrack

## Who Is That Dog?

A makeover like Samantha's is worthy of its own reality show, as is portrayed on Judith's layout featuring her sheepdog's "Big Reveal." Judith juxtaposed the before and after photos of grooming day and set them over angled strips of papers and cardstock that play on the pointed silhouette of scissors. She painted her title letter stickers and added large, hand-cut question marks to pull the page together with cheerful colors and playful patterns.

Judith Mara, Lancaster, Massachusetts

**Supplies:** Patterned paper (Pebbles); ribbon (Michaels); letter stickers (Creative Imaginations); photo corners (Making Memories); thread; acrylic paint; sewing machine

## Poki's Top 10

While there are so many reasons to enjoy a spring day at the dog park, on this page, Poki limits her list to her top 10. Stephanie often uses list-style journaling in her pet layouts to keep the journaling simple but memorable, while also adding humor. She designed her funky title around an oversized button that doubles as a playful embellishment to allow room for the large photo of Poki in her element.

Stephanie Milner, Ventura, California

**Supplies:** Patterned paper (Scenic Route Paper Co.); textured cardstock, oversized button (Bazzill); letter stickers (Memories Complete); ribbon (Offray); buttons (Wal-Mart); eyelets; pens

## Color My World

Although Mary was excited to experiment with a roll of black-and-white film, the images of her two redheaded felines seemed lifeless without their trademark color. Mary expresses in her journaling block how the colorful personalities of these two furry little guys bring so much vibrant life into her household that black-and-white film could never do them justice. As a result, she used a joyful palette of colors and patterns in this epiphany page to celebrate the ways her fiery-haired felines color her world.

Mary Fontana Burke, Franklin, Tennessee

**Supplies:** Patterned papers (Chatterbox); ribbon (May Arts); mini brads (Lasting Impressions); metal corners (Making Memories); letter charms (Karen Foster Design); chipboard letters (Li'l Davis Designs); stamping ink; pen

*In August, I decided to experiment with black and white film—something I had not done in years. I was not exactly thrilled when I got the roll developed. While the photos were interesting to view, something was definitely missing! I realized that these little guys bring so much to our household—joy, laughter, beauty, mischief, activity, companionship—and these things are all colorful! Color processing just seems to come a little bit closer to capturing their cuteness on film. I love these adorable red-headed fellars!*

2004

**Cats** have been **domesticated** for **half as long as dogs** have been.

# a frog, a toad and a turtle

Imagine putting a toddler, an 8 year old boy and a grumpy old man in a very small living space and that's basically the world of Willy, Freddie and Hank. You get quite an array of personalities with these three. Willy the turtle is like a toddler still trying to figure out the aquarium he lives in. Freddie is a young, energetic frog who seems to be free spirited and always on the go. But Hank is the one with the real personality. A toad who looks just like a grumpy old man, Hank lives up to that first impression. His frown is permanent, and it's pretty clear that most days he's thinking "What do YOU want?" Even though these three are completely different personalities, they are a ton of fun for Drake and Elsie. Sometimes it's a little bit like "Wild Kingdom" but making these animals a part of our home was a great way to introduce the kids to the world beyond the dog and the cat. Who knew such ugly little things could become part of the family?

## A Frog, a Toad and a Turtle

These three wee friends may share the same living space, but their personalities are completely different, as Courtney's lively and lush layout describes. Each atypical pet is featured individually in the lower right corner, balancing out the journaling block on the page, while a large photo of the reptilian trio fills the upper portion of the design. Coordinating buttons in amphibious colors bring texture and dimension to the page, while emphasizing the trio's look and feel.

Courtney Walsh, Winnebago, Illinois

**Supplies:** Patterned paper (Arctic Frog); textured cardstock (Bazzill); buttons (Junkitz); embroidery floss (DMC); ribbon (source unknown); staples; transparency

**Frogs** can **jump 20 times their body length.** The **longest** frog jump on record measured **33 feet, 5.5 inches.**

# NAUGHTY

Tigger, at times you are truly testing our patience! Once Jeremy and I are home and you are not in the same room as we are, you will make yourself heard! It starts out with meowing. If that doesn't work, you will move your paws along the door and the last resort is to run towards the door and to throw yourself with your entire body against the door, which results in a loud BANG. Once you are out and in the same room as we are, you are a little cuddle monster!

# OR NICE?

## Naughty or Nice?

The mesmerizing gaze from Tigger's green eyes expresses the determination of this dual-personality cat to be close to the ones he loves. Sybille's complementary-colored design incorporates striped patterned papers to play up Tigger's tangerine fur, while masses of fibers tied through plastic washers add dimension and spunk to the page. Her journaling, printed over three stacked tags on a transparency, tells of Tigger's Dr. Jekyll/Mr. Hyde transformation the moment his owners arrive home.

Sybille Moen, Tarzana, California

**Supplies:** Patterned paper (Junkitz); fibers (Basic Grey); letter stamps (Altered Paper Press, Li'l Davis Designs); washers (Bazzill); solvent ink (Tsukineko); transparency; shipping tags; ribbon

## It's a Dog's Life

An accordion-style mini book serves as an informative addition to Tristann's page featuring her cherished greyhound, Amie. A photo turn holds the booklet in place, which is adorned with ribbons tied through eyelets and black letter brads. For additional texture reminiscent of Amie's coat, Tristann created a playful word embellishment by threading a strip of paper through woven loop letters, which she attached to the matted photo with brads.

Tristann Graves, Vancouver, Washington

**Supplies:** Patterned paper, woven letter accents, metal letter brads (Carolee's Creations); textured cardstock (Bazzill); dog-themed stickers (EK Success); eyelets, metal-rimmed tag, photo turns (Making Memories); mini brads (American Tag Co.); ribbon (EK Success, Offray); square paper clip (source unknown); cardstock; pen

# Colbalt

Although peacocks are typically afraid of dogs, Colbalt seems to believe he is a canine trapped in a bird's body. Pullout tags adorned with stapled ribbons artfully mimic the look of Colbalt's plumage and reveal the comical story of how he adopted himself into Mary's family, joining their brood of six dogs. Circle-print paper plays up the patterns in Colbalt's feathers while solid teal cardstock portrays his beautiful shade of blue. A pullout tag from the center of the photo pocket displays a close-up of Colbalt in all his feathered (though he would prefer it furry) glory.

Mary Hager,
Bainbridge Island, Washington

**Supplies:** Patterned paper (Basic Grey); cardstock tags (7 Gypsies); ribbon, photo anchors (Making Memories); metal tag (Limited Edition Rubberstamps); ribbon; cardstock; brads, staples

## Dog Said Cat Said

A conversation between Katie's cat and dog provides humorous insight into the relationship and rivalry between these two "siblings." The surreal effect of Katie's photos was formed by using photo-editing software to change her original prints to black-and-white. She then printed the augmented photo onto a transparency, as well as dialogue representative of both pets.

**Katie Harkins, Ottawa, Ontario, Canada**

**Supplies:** Patterned paper (Basic Grey); image-editing software (Adobe Photoshop); ribbon; transparency

A **cat's brain** is more **similar** to a **human's brain** than that of a dog's.

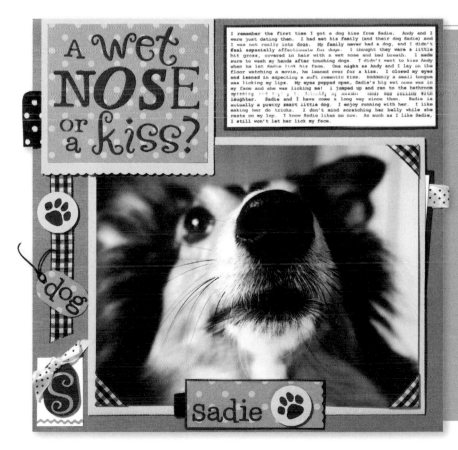

## A Wet Nose or a Kiss?

Sadie loves to give kisses, and Karyn snapped this photo just in time as Sadie was sniffing the camera with an amorous look! She used a large photo and prominent title treatment as the main attractions of the layout and complemented the design with ribbons and die-cut accents. To help convey Sadie's sassy side, Karyn chose preppy polka dots and plaids and created bows, bands and photo corners as well as a pull for further images tucked behind the focal photo.

**Karyn Nicoll for QuicKutz, Chicago, Illinois**

**Supplies:** Patterned paper (Lasting Impressions); textured cardstock (Bazzill); ribbons (Wal-Mart); die-cut letters, dog tag, and paw print (QuicKutz); foam adhesive spacers

FURRY FELINE FRIEND FUN

Name: Socks
Nicknames: Sock-a-Pooh, Poo, Poo-man-choo
Color: Black and white
Eyes: Yellow/Green
Sex: Male
Birthplace: Virginia
Age: 3
Sock got his name obviously because of his white paws. He is very loving and tolerant of his humans picking him up and loving all over him. His favorite pastime is making Rat hiss.

Socks

# Socks and Rat

Dar designed this two-page spread to share the vital statistics of her two favorite felines, Socks and Rat. Each page features a close-up image of the featured furry friend and lists key information such as place of birth, names, colors and personality traits. Dar created a file folder for each cat with the name placed in the tab portion, a sticker replica of each and ribbon for embellishment. Each page is designed as a reverse image from top to bottom of the other, with torn paper edges and inked borders.

Dar Kaso, Virginia Beach, Virginia

**Supplies:** Patterned paper (Daisy D's); ribbon, rub-on words (Making Memories); cat stickers (EK Success); file folders (Pinecone Press); cardstock; stamping ink

Rat

Name: Rat
Nicknames: Ratta, Mrs. Ratty
Color: White
Eyes: Yellow/Green
Sex: Female
Birthplace: Hawaii
Age: 11
We named her Rat because when we got her she was so tiny and when gave her a bath she looked just like a little white rat. She has the sweetest pink ears and nose. Rat hates to be picked up, she comes to you when she wants attention. She loves to sleep in my bed and be left alone to do cat things.

**Cats** step with both left legs, then both right legs when they walk or run. The only other animals to do this are the **giraffe and the camel.**

FURRY FELINE FRIEND FUN

## Snuggle-Pants

When I agreed to watch Nigel for a couple of months while Warren and Linda moved to Calgary, I had no idea what I was in for! I had never owned a cat before, and really was not a cat fan. He kind of grew on me, though, and when Linda called a few months later asking if I would keep Nigel, I happily said I would. Nigel has turned out to be very much a dog in cat's clothing. Independent, he is not! He stands on the bed and cries at the top of his lungs until someone comes upstairs to cuddle with him. At night, he sleeps right between Dave and I, or on top of one of us. He loves to have skin-to-paw contact, and there have been more than one morning that I've woken up with him on my chest, with both paws on my cheeks, purring contentedly. This kind of behaviour has earned him the nickname of snuggle-pants because that seems to be what he wears all the time. He was definitely not what I expected from a cat, and I love him for it!

## Snuggle Pants

Nigel is not your typical cat—and Colleen loves him for it! With no signs of an independent attitude, all this sweet tabby wants to do is snuggle or cuddle night and day. Colleen's husband captured this photo of Nigel's loving nature by using a lamp aimed at the side and no flash to avoid the dreaded "cat eye" glare. Colleen created this layout using her computer, forming the background paper by taking a brown sample image of the cat's fur and then applying a stained-glass filter to it. She then applied a craquelure filter and a gaussian blur filter to obtain the warm glow.

Colleen Yoshida, Cold Lake, Alberta, Canada
Photo: David Yoshida, Cold Lake, Alberta, Canada

Supplies: Image-editing software (Adobe Photoshop 7.0)

## Pet Memorabilia

- Certificate of adoption
- Certificate of obedience training
- Registration papers
- Baby teeth
- Paw prints and impressions
- Food labels
- Identification tags
- Veterinary documents
- First collar
- Lists of firsts and special accomplishments
- Tufts of fur/feathers

# Mocha

Despite the innocent look on Mocha's face, she is quite the "spirited child," or has "personality plus" as Katie's family likes to put it. The brilliant choice of colors and energetic patterns personify Mocha's *je ne sais quoi*, which makes her a much-exhausting, yet definitely much-loved bundle of spunk. Katie downloaded all of her papers and elements to pull together this vibrant computer-generated tribute.

Katie Pertiet, Naperville, Illinois

**Supplies:** Patterned papers (Run Spot Run Paper Pack, www.designerdigitals.com); letter tiles, stitching, twill (www.designerdigitals.com)

# Best Friend

After losing her precious dog of 12 years, Melanie asked for Jasmine the dachshund to help heal her heart. Melanie created this page to pay tribute to Jasmine's faithful friendship, capturing her kindness and understanding through the sincere expressions in each photo. Melanie mounted her focal photo atop a classified ad-style patterned paper and used chalk ink to highlight Jasmine's breed. Melanie added stitching detail around the edges of the vellum quote for a tender, homespun touch.

Melanie Douthit, West Monroe, Louisiana

**Supplies:** Patterned papers, cardstock stickers, vellum quote (Flair Designs); chalk ink (Clearsnap)

# {snow} boots

On April 10th, 2005 my step mom, Debbie, emailed these photos that were taken during a blizzard that shut down Denver and a few towns around it. Her email read: "It was short-sleeve weather yesterday, upper 60's. But the weathermen were right, and it started snowing early this morning. We have 15 inches now and it is still falling. We had to go out to shake the heavy, wet snow off the tree branches to help prevent them from snapping off."

"Thankfully, we found Ilka's old snowsuit for Riley. He was running and hopping through snow much deeper than he is tall as he followed Pete into the backyard and huge snowballs formed on his exposed legs. Without the coat he would have been one big snowball! We had to wash the snowballs off under warm water to thaw him out!"

## Snow Boots

Decked out in a bright red snowsuit, Candice's dog, Riley, ventured outside into blizzard conditions and returned indoors with snowballs covering his legs like boots! Candice ran the large photo of Riley across both pages and then overlapped it on the right page with cropped photos that further illustrate the massive snowfall. She printed her journaling in a festive font directly onto the cardstock and added letter and accent stickers to lighten up the look with winter-white fun.

Candice Cruz, Somerville, Massachusetts
Photo: Debbie Cruz, Aurora, Colorado

**Supplies:** Letter and star stickers (American Crafts); cardstock

The **traditional pompom poodle haircut** was originally developed to increase the poodles' swimming abilities as retrievers. The shaved cut allowed for **faster swimming** while the distinctive pompoms were left to keep the joints warm.

## Impressions
## of a Cat

While Katja's kitty may strut around with a majestic air, he's really just a big softy looking for a tummy rub. Katja's layout features two large images of her split-personality cat looking regal and refined, while the central photo at the bottom unveils his inner cuddle-bug begging for attention. Katja created the collar embellishment by adhering eyelets and snaps to a ribbon and adding a buckle from an old luggage tag. She topped it off with a tag created from a photo turn set over a metal-rimmed monogram tag.

**Katja Kromann, Mission Viejo, California**

**Supplies:** Patterned papers, hand-dyed silk, rub-on letters, twill stickers (Paper House Productions); textured cardstock (Bazzill); metal-rimmed circle tag, snaps, eyelets (Making Memories); photo turn (Jest Charming); luggage tag buckle

## Remmy Blue Eyes

Remmy's sky blue eyes take center stage on Nicole's cool and collected layout that expresses the gentle, laid-back attitude of her tabby boy. She used a coordinating blue background and cool-colored papers to feature Remmy's baby blues. Chipboard letters add dimension and shine, while acrylic eyelets crossed with fiber mimic the shape of those piercing peepers. Nicole personalized a paint chip by adding a rub-on circle to the showcased hue in addition to rub-on letters.

**Nicole Keller, Rio Hondo, Texas**

**Supplies:** Patterned papers (KI Memories, Scrapbook Trends); textured cardstock (DieCuts with a View); chipboard letter tiles (Li'l Davis Designs); rub-on letters (Chatterbox); rub-on circles (KI Memories); acrylic letters (Hobby Lobby); mini brad, flower brad (Making Memories); fibers (Fiber Accents); acrylic eyelets (Paperbilities); paint chip (Daisy D's)

# Bruce

Wanting to feature "the scoop" on Bruce the Cat on a single layout, Corine chronicled this crazy cat's qualities and quirks in a question/answer, interview-style format. Corine cropped several images that accentuate her feisty feline's distinctive features and adhered them to the front of folded cardstock that opens to reveal a close-up. Bits of frayed denim lend a tattered and tough feel to the page and incorporate the look of Bruce's favorite pastime—shredding things! Corine treated her cardstock with paint prior to printing her journaling for an urban touch.

Corine Smitt, Alphen aan den Rijn, The Netherlands

**Supplies:** Patterned paper (Imagination Project); textured cardstock (Bazzill); foam letter stamps, brass photo turns, rub-on letters, colored staples (Making Memories); die-cut circles (QuicKutz); solvent ink (Tsukineko); snaps, stickers, mini tags (source unknown); acrylic paint; denim

# Satchel's 10 Commandments

When Carmel found this clever poem, she instantly wanted to create a page around it in honor of His Royal Highness, Satchel the cat. Carmel slightly altered the wording of the poem in order to tailor it to her cat's personality. She kept the look of the page simple, using clean lines and minimal embellishments to allow the photo to reign as the supreme focus. Carmel cleverly established the look of a collar by wrapping ribbon around the striped lower paper band and threading it through an oval tag.

Carmel Flores, Westfield, Indiana

**Supplies:** Patterned papers (EK Success); ribbon (Offray); rub-on numbers (Scrapworks); cardstock; chipboard

1. I am the Lord of thy house.
2. Thou shall have no other pets before me.
3. Thou shalt not ever ignore me
4. I shall ignore thou when I feel like it.
5. Thou shalt be grateful that I even give thou the time of day.
6. Remember my food dish and keep it full.
7. Thou shalt spend most of thy money on toys and gifts for me.
8. Thou shalt always have thy lap ready for me to curl up in.
9. Thou shalt shower me with love and attention upon demand.
10. Above all thou shalt do anything and everything it takes to keep me happy.

# Scooby-Doo

This calico beauty got her name by the way she would run at top speed into the room whenever the popular cartoon's theme song began! When Cindi found these rich and sophisticated pet-themed papers and stickers, she just had to design a layout around her Scooby-Doo. She combined the background papers with coordinating cardstocks and embellishments and antiqued the ribbons with walnut ink to meld with the tones in the papers. The top layer of cardstock on the right was scored to fold back and reveal how Scooby joined the family and the ways her gentle spirit has brought them joy.

Cindi Bisson, Clayton, North Carolina

**Supplies:** Patterned paper, pet-themed stickers (Karen Foster Design); textured cardstock (Bazzill); button-hole strip, burlap edge stickers (Sweetwater); letter stamps (Purple Onion Designs); mini brads, colored safety pins (Magic Scraps); rusted tin heart (Primitive Barn); cat paw punch (Punch Bunch); fish button, fibers, burlap, ribbons (source unknown); deckle scissors (Fiskars); walnut ink (Keepsake Designs); cardstock; acrylic paint; foam adhesive spacers

### OUR LITTLE SCOOBY-DOO

Scooby joined our family almost 20 years ago. The first time I ever saw her she was so tiny she fit in the palm of my hand. Scooby was born in a dairy barn in Wolcott, VT. Our friend Dave Greene's family owned the farm – and Pa Greene told us that she was the only multi-colored kitten he ever remembered being born there. She was too young to come home the first day, but Pa promised to try to keep her safe until she was six weeks old. We returned at that time and there she was safe and sound. They told us she had a close call when a cow stepped on her but Pa saved her in time. We brought her home and Tigger fell in love. He adopted her and treated her like HE was her mother. It was so sweet. They became best kitty friends. Baby Doll wasn't as thrilled, but she tolerated her. Originally, her name was Scruffy but that just didn't seem to fit. I used to watch the old Scooby Doo cartoons and every time the music would start she'd come running and sit in front of the TV so I started calling her Scooby-Doo and the name just stuck.

Scooby is the most lovable, sweet, cuddly, patient and gentle cat I have ever known. She loves to have her belly rubbed and just loves to sleep with the boys – especially on their pillows wrapped around their heads. No matter what they do to her she never scratches or bites. She loves to fetch fur mice. Story time with the boys is her favorite time of day for cuddling. Her only annoying habit is that when she is really happy she DROOLS like mad so Darrin calls her Drooly Doo. She isn't thrilled about her newly adopted sister Sunshine – in fact she's afraid of the kitten – but she tolerates her and doesn't try to harm her. Just another example of her gentle nature.

She's a good girl and we are so happy that she has been part of our family for so many years. We love you Scooby-Doo.

– November, 2004

## Year of the Rooster

Carolyn's cat, Squeaker, has always had the nickname "Rooster." So when the Chinese New Year—Year of the Rooster rolled around, she found it the perfect opportunity to pay extra-special tribute to her favorite feline! Carolyn set the backdrop for Squeaker's page using rooster-patterned paper and included history on the Chinese New Year in her journaling block. By adding Oriental stickers, a Chinese New Year postage stamp and a Chinese coin, this all-American cat embraces his namesake year with true Asian flair.

**Carolyn Cleveland, Maysville, Georgia**

**Supplies:** Patterned paper (Scenic Route Paper Co.); textured cardstocks (Bazzill); ribbons (May Arts); die-cut rooster (Paper House Productions); die-cut letters (Foofala); letter stickers (Club Scrap, Provo Craft); coin (Club Scrap); postage stamp, stamping ink

## I Love My Cat

Posing for the camera is second nature to Felix, whose debonair nature is showcased on Christine's layout. She altered this photo resulting from a shoot she did with Felix to sepia using photo-editing software. Christine filled Felix's page with favorite pastimes and playthings to personalize the tribute, including stickers of toys, belts and ribbons. The crown set behind the photo conveys a sense of royalty and adds an even more regal look to Felix's photo.

**Christine Traversa, Joliet, Illinois**

**Supplies:** Patterned paper, pet themed stickers (Karen Foster Design); diamond background stamp (Stamps Happen); ribbons (May Arts, Michaels); crown accent (Foofala); image-editing software (Kodak); stamping ink; acrylic paints

In relation to their body size, **cats** have the **largest eyes** of any mammal.

# Buford

A series of endearing black-and-white images express the sweetness of Angela's wrinkly pup, Buford. She used one regal-looking headshot for her focal photo on each page, and then used a series of three cropped images to highlight Buford's many expressions. Earthy tones of red and green patterned papers and buttons lend a masculine flair to the spread, while a coordinating plaid adds a sense of energy and playfulness. Angela softened the look of the cheery plaid by adding a printed pet-themed vellum overlay to each page.

Angela Moen, Casco, Maine

**Supplies:** Patterned paper (Daisy D's); textured cardstock (Bazzill); decorative vellum (Boxer Scrapbook Productions); buttons (SEI); ribbon (Offray); eyelets (Making Memories); epoxy letters (Li'l Davis Designs); stamping ink; thread; mini tags

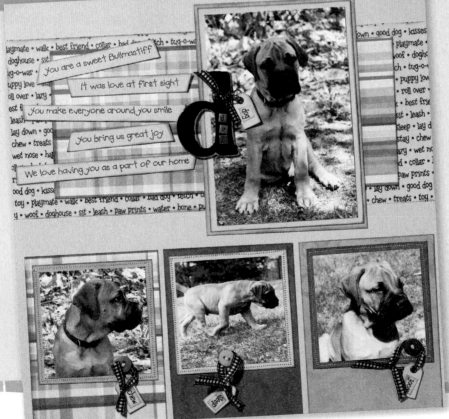

## She's Got Such Great (Dane) Style

Posing for the camera with such exaggerated expressions and movements is all part of Daphne the Great Dane's irresistible style. Silk flowers and ribbons lend bohemian beauty to Pam's fashionable layout, detailing Daphne's signature look. A watch face embellishment, sleek silver brads and a regal stamped title give the page a glamorous air, while a vertical arrangement of letter tags set on edge lends artsy attitude.

**Pam Callaghan, Bowling Green, Ohio**

**Supplies:** Patterned paper, printed circle elements (Chatterbox); textured cardstock (Bazzill); ribbons (Li'l Davis Designs, May Arts), rub-on letters, brads, magnetic stamps (Making Memories); watch face (Jest Charming); rub-on letters (Imagination Project); circle tag letters (Outdoors & More Scrapbook Decor); walnut ink (Ranger); stamping ink; silk flowers, staples

## Sammy

This tiny bundle of joy is a big snuggler and just loves to be cuddled by her family. Jamie made this page to feature this precious, palm-sized princess and all her adorable puppy parts. The illusion of bulky embellishments was created through E-Cuts, which Jamie personally designed using a puppy motif and then simply downloaded and printed. The collaged tags, journaling block and even the distressed edges are all electronic die cuts, making for a quick and easy page with a big impact.

**Jamie Harper, Phoenix, Arizona**

**Supplies:** Patterned paper, letter stamps (Rusty Pickle); textured cardstock (Bazzill); tags, journaling box E-Cuts (www.scrapbook.com); solvent ink (Tsukineko)

The **largest breed** of dog is the **Irish wolfhound,** which can weigh up to 150 pounds. The **smallest breed,** the **Chihuahua,** can weigh as little as 2 pounds.

# Mattie's Extreme Makeover

This layout documents how the matted, moppy-haired mess that followed Tish and her husband home one day was transformed into a beautiful belle and much-loved family member. Using vintage-style patterned papers as inspiration, Tish incorporated a combination of faux and real leather accents to adorn her endearing diamond-in-the-"ruff" page. To achieve the look of leather for the mini book, Tish soaked cardstock in water for 10 minutes, wrung it out, and then pressure stamped it to make the impressions in the paper. Once dried, she antiqued the paper with chalk and applied a layer of acrylic varnish over the top.

Tish Rogers, Cambria, California

**Supplies:** Patterned papers (Design Originals); dog print stamp (Stamp Cabana); Cocker stamp (All Night Media); brads (Making Memories); fiber (EK Success); glass beads (Bead Heaven); dog bone charm, tags (Card Connection, Hirschberg, Schutz & Co.); dog paw sticker (PSX Design); cardstock; eyelets; foam adhesive spacers; chalk; leather strip; sandpaper; acrylic varnish

# My Greatest Love

Love is always the greatest gift, and that's exactly what Kerry received for her 21st birthday when Maximus unwrapped her heart. To convey the loving and giving disposition of her treasured pup, Kerry used a solid red background and accentuated it with a printed love-themed transparency and strips and punches from patterned papers. The bottle cap letters used in her title, as well as the metal corners, brads and letter charm, all lend a masculine edge to the page through their industrial-looking appeal.

Kerry Layman, Monroe, Georgia

**Supplies:** Patterned paper (Bo-Bunny Press, Daisy D's); textured cardstock (Bazzill); printed transparency (Creative Imaginations); bottle cap letters (Li'l Davis Designs); metal corners, metal clips, metal letter, brads, clear definition stickers (Making Memories); cardstock

## True Love

Puppy love in the truest sense is illustrated on this father/pup pug page. Here Colleen used reds, golds and black to design a love-themed, masculine-looking layout that still combines the colors found in the dogs' fur. Printed fabric, ribbons, buttons and wooden accents establish a combination of all that is tender and tough. By cutting the top black ribbon to a point and adorning it with eyelets, Colleen created the look of a collar, to which she added a ball chain with dangling love-themed tags.

Colleen Adams, Huntington Beach, California
Photo: Chase Fedderson, Huntington Beach, California

**Supplies:** Patterned paper (Club Scrap); ribbons (May Arts, Offray); ball chain, eyelets, metal tags (Making Memories); wooden letters, frame (Li'l Davis Designs); letter stamps (PSX Design); letter sticker (Creative Imaginations); photo corners (Canson); buttons; fabric

## Who Needs 101... When We Have This 1?

The woeful look on Marcia's pooch's face always melts away and turns to cheer to welcome the family home. Marcia created this page to show how loved her pouting pup is without even trying. She punched squares of coordinating patterned papers to create a retro style background prior to adding the other page elements. Dog-themed buttons provide dimensional charm, while Dalmation-themed stamps illustrate the title and create a visual doggy treat.

Marcia Steeves, Peterborough, Ontario, Canada

**Supplies:** Patterned paper (Chatterbox, Top Line Creations); letter stickers (Top Line Creations); die-cut letters (Sizzix); rubber stamps (Disney Company); metal-rimmed tag, brad, ribbon (Making Memories); dog-themed buttons (Buttons Galore); vellum; cardstock; stamping ink; embossing powder; foam adhesive spacers

## Grandma's Kitty

Although Anna Marie's grandmother isn't a "cat person," upon a recent visit, Grandma and Bandit bonded nonetheless thanks to their similar sweet and gentle dispositions. Anna Marie used Christmas patterned paper to play up the colors of Bandit's eyes and the sticker seen in the photo. She embellished the design by tying coordinating ribbons through buttonhole twill, which tied to the look of the woven letters in the title.

Anna Marie DeHaven, Poquoson, Virginia

**Supplies:** Patterned papers, twill buttonhole ribbon, twill letters, metal word charm, cardstock stickers, metal letter brads (Carolee's Creations); ribbons (Bazzill, Making Memories, May Arts)

## Who Would Have Guessed?

Despite the stereotype of being "icky and disgusting," Cheddar the rat is a sensitive, smart, sweet and silly rodent who has found a home in Michelle's family. Using numerous rub-on letters in different fonts and colors, Michelle listed Cheddar's charming personality traits in addition to other layered words in her title element. She used a circle punch to pull colored circles from her patterned paper and staggered them about the left side for balance. A unique copper flower accent dresses up the title element, which mimics the appearance of a wheel of cheese!

Michelle Tardie, Richmond, Virginia

**Supplies:** Patterned paper, photo turns, brad (Making Memories); rub-on letters (Creative Imaginations, Imagination Project, Making Memories); metal flower (Nunn Design); photo corner (Canson); circle punch (EK Success); circle template (Provo Craft)

## Many Moods of Max

Camille's playful parrot, Max, steals the show on this layout that highlights his many moods. By downloading colorful words onto her photos using a digital kit, Camille created comedic captions for each of Max's personality traits. Camille created her own patterned paper to perfectly match Max's colors by using coordinating crayons on white cardstock and then painting over it with acrylic paint. She then scratched the feather designs onto the coated paper with a paper clip and embellished the look with actual feathers Max had lost over the course of the year.

Camille Bennett, Fremont, California

Supplies: Textured cardstocks (Bazzill); printed letters on photos (Reflections of Friends Digital Kit, www.amyjosmith.com); letter stamps (River City Rubber Works, Stamp Craft); crayons (Crayola); acrylic paint; ribbon; feathers

ANY MOODS OF MAX

CuDDLy

I'm not sure what we were thinking when we bought MAX. Bringing a baby parrot into our home just months before our own baby arrived seems crazy now. When I came across the picture of Max & his sister for sale on Craigslist, I couldn't pass up the opportunity to go meet these.

6 months old

Poicephalus meyeri matschiei

PLayfuL

SILLY

Entertaining

Meyer's Parrot (blue-rumped)

**Parakeets**, a member of the parrot family, are **monogamous**. In the wild, once they find **a mate, it is for life.**

## Up Close and Personal

This up-close image of Mr. Beer, Jen's beloved furry family member, inspired her to create an insightful page on his extremely "in-your-face" personality. Jen kept the page design simple to allow the large photo to maintain the focus of the layout and added a small charm frame beneath filled with a photo from her index print sheet. For a final touch, Jen added ribbons and a metal spiral accent for added interest.

Jen Carlson, Vacaville, California

Photo: Christa Krupski, Kirksville, Missouri

**Supplies:** Patterned papers (Imagination Project, Junkitz, SEI); textured cardstock (Bazzill); rub-on letters (Making Memories); mini-frame charm (K & Company); metal spiral (7 Gypsies); ribbons (Offray, Stampin' Up!)

# Tips for Top-Notch Pet Photos

• **Select the correct film:** For action shots of your pet, choose a faster film such as ISO 400 or 800 to avoid a blurry effect. For relatively still shots, use a slower speed film such as 100 or 200.

• **Avoid using a flash:** To keep your pet's eyes from assuming a glow, photograph him or her indoors by a window using natural light or outside in a shady spot. To capture the details of solid-colored fur, position your pet so that the light source comes from the side to emphasize definition and texture. Consider using a large sheet of white cardboard as a reflector to indirectly project light onto your pet.

• **Consider your backdrop:** Photograph your pets outdoors for a beautiful natural landscape or capture them in their favorite spots around the house where they may be most comfortable.

• **Be patient:** Don't attempt to force your pet to pose, and be prepared to take several shots in order to get one or two great photos. You may be able to elicit an endearing head tilt or set of perked ears by making a noise or saying key phrases that appeal to your pet.

• **Make it fun:** Hold a treat or toy to encourage your pet to look in the desired direction, then reward him for his cooperation. Photo shoots may just become a favorite game!

• **Experiment with perspective:** Shoot from several different angles, such as eye-level, from below, directly above or from the side of your subject. Don't be afraid to fill the frame to capture the details of your pet.

• **Prep your pet:** For more portrait-style photos, bathe and groom your pet so that she looks her best.

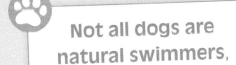

## I Am an Indoor Dog!

Despite numerous attempts to embrace her inner Labrador, Barb's dog, Olive, sets the record straight on this hilarious two-page spread which stresses through a letter from Olive's perspective that she is NOT an outdoor dog. Barb created the look of splashing water around photos of Olive by color washing white cardstock with paper dyes. The journaling was created by running looseleaf paper through a printer, crumpling it, scanning it and printing it onto cardstock for the effect of wrinkled notebook paper while remaining perfectly flat.

Barb Hogan, Cincinnati, Ohio

**Supplies:** Textured cardstocks (Bazzill); paper dyes (The Scrapbooking Society); letter stickers (Li'l Davis Designs, Wordsworth); decorative brads, metal letters (Making Memories); metal frame charm, label stickers (Pebbles); fiber

**Not all dogs are natural swimmers**, nor do all dogs love to be in the water. **Many require gradual training** to build their confidence and ability to **stay afloat.**

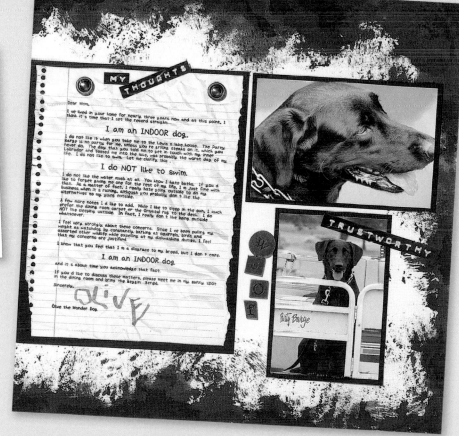

**pals**

Companion
Friend
Playmate
Comrade
Buddy

**Wet Wipe**

Nathan and Loki    June 2005

# chapter four | Pets and Their Favorite People

The longer you come to know and love your pet, the more you wonder, "Exactly who adopted whom?" Our animals see and love us for who we truly are, flaws and all, and offer us loyalty and comfort without hesitation. And while we invest our time into training our pets, they teach us so much in the process: how to love unconditionally, how to be comfortable in our skin, and how to find beauty in bulging eyes, wrinkly round bodies, under-bites and out-of-control fur. But most of all, pets teach us what it means to be a companion. Commemorate the bond you share on scrapbook pages that celebrate the ways your mutual lives have been enriched.

## Teddy Bear

Almost as cuddly as a real teddy bear, Amy's daughter's hamster is her very special and snuggly companion. This layout celebrates the unique bond these two friends share, featuring photos of Teddy Bear taking food from Megan's fingers, snuggling in her hands, and just sitting close by to listen. All patterned papers and page elements were downloaded from the Internet to create this computer-generated design. Photo-editing software and a free plug-in enhanced the soft, sweet images.

Amy Edwards, Newark Valley, New York

**Supplies:** Image-editing software (Adobe Photoshop CS); plug-in (Virtual Photography); patterned paper (www.scrapbookgraphics.com); torn overlay (Steph, scrapbook-bytes .com); "adorable" word (Rhonna Farrer, www.twopeasin abucket.com); remaining digital elements (Jen Wilson, www. scrapbook-bytes.com)

Teddy Bear is one of the loves of Megan's little life! She loves him to pieces and spends quite a bit of time with him; whenever she can! Several times a day in fact. He stands at the cage waiting for her to let him out. He loves to gather food from her finger tips - they have a VERY loving relationship ~2005

NOTES: A small Eurasian rodent of the subfamily Cricetinae, especially Mesocricetus auratus, having large cheek pouches and a short tail and often kept as a pet.

---

Olivia with Prissy on a summer day....just hanging out. When Olivia saw this photo, she was a little miffed. Her first comment was "Oh, Prissy closed her eyes!", as if Prissy knew she was being photographed, and did it on purpose. 5 seconds after the shot, Prissy popped Olivia on the cheek with her soft paw saying "I want down NOW". She's usually not so irritable. Maybe she just didn't like the pose. May. 2005

These are the days we will remember...

## Summer Days

Enjoying the cat-days of summer, Olivia and Prissy stopped for a quick photo op on a beautiful day...even if Prissy was less than thrilled about it. According to Angelia's journaling, when this photo was being taken, Prissy really wanted to be doing her own thing. To unify the dynamic look of the stark white journaling section with the patterned paper title element, Angelia used a wide twill band around a chipboard frame, which she fastened into place with brads to attach to the journaling block.

Angelia Wigginton, Belmont, Mississippi

**Supplies:** Patterned papers (Arctic Frog, KI Memories); textured cardstock (Bazzill); chipboard frame (Li'l Davis Designs); embossed sticker, title stickers (Making Memories); twill (May Arts); brads (Karen Foster Design)

## New Best Friend

Every little girl needs a kitten to cuddle up with. After Ki's daughter, Presley, brought home Waldo, a forever friendship was formed that is celebrated on this layout. Ki gave the page a fun yet classic look, playing up the theme of blossoming friendship through flower accents and vintage prints, complemented by the frill of ribbons.

**Ki Kruk, Sherwood Park, Alberta, Canada**

**Supplies:** Patterned papers, letter stickers, rub-on phrase, file tabs (SEI); ribbon (Morex Corp., SEI); rivet (Chatterbox); colored staples, flower brads (Making Memories); square brads (Creative Impressions); silk flower

## Flower

For a fun page addition, Summer incorporated into her layout a drawing her child did of their beloved cat, Flower. She mounted the mini masterpiece onto black cardstock, along with a photo of the muse beside it. For a timeless, tender touch, Summer used machine-stitching around both elements. A transparent definition sticker placed over the stamped title letters adds visual appeal, while a single metal cat charm lends shine and pizazz.

**Summer Ford, Bulverde, Texas**

**Supplies:** Patterned paper, fiber (Basic Grey); metal-rimmed tag (Making Memories); definition stickers (EK Success); cat charm (source unknown); foam letter stamps (Li'l Davis Designs, Making Memories); cardstock; date stamp; pen; acrylic paint; stamping ink

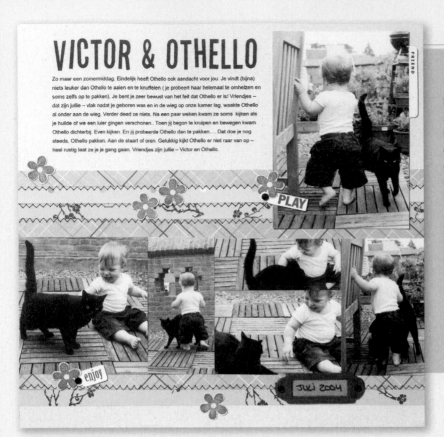

# VICTOR & OTHELLO

Zo maar een zomermiddag. Eindelijk heeft Othello ook aandacht voor jou. Je vindt (bijna) niets leuker dan Othello te aaien en te knuffelen ( je probeert haar helemaal te omhelzen en soms zelfs op te pakken). Je bent je zeer bewust van het feit dat Othello er is! Vriendjes – dat zijn jullie – vlak nadat je geboren was en in de wieg op onze kamer lag, waakte Othello al onder aan de wieg. Verder deed ze niets. Na een paar weken kwam ze soms kijken als je huilde of we een luier gingen verschonen. Toen jij begon te kruipen en bewegen kwam Othello dichterbij. Even kijken. En jij probeerde Othello dan te pakken…. Dat doe je nog steeds, Othello pakken. Aan de staart of oren. Gelukkig kijkt Othello er niet raar van op – heel rustig laat ze je je gang gaan. Vriendjes zijn jullie – Victor en Othello.

PLAY

enjoy

JULI 2004

## Victor and Othello

Florence's layout utilizes serene colors and soft, playful accents to feature her son's purr-fect friendship with their cat, Othello. The cheery flower notions were stamped, cut out and placed whimsically about the page, establishing a sense of movement and a light-heartedness to mimic the cat's behavior in the photos. Florence attached printed file tabs with black brads to several of the photos and set a leather label holder at the bottom to showcase the date with a touch of masculine flair.

Florence Bavinck, The Netherlands

**Supplies:** Patterned paper (KI Memories, Mara-Mi); flower stamps (Stampin' Up!); leather label holder (Making Memories); index synonym tags (Autumn Leaves); brads; stamping ink; sewing machine

If a **cat rolls over** on her back and exposes her belly, **it** means **she trusts you.**

## Bowser

What little girl wouldn't like to have an oversized teddy bear to love on? Lisa's daughter, Danielle, is one such lucky young lady, and Bowser doesn't seem to mind one bit! Lisa created a cheerful design using coordinating pet papers and page accents in colors that complement her photos. For a little dimension, Lisa created a title treatment comprised of painted metal stencil letters.

Lisa Turley, Chesapeake, Virginia

**Supplies:** Patterned paper and accents (Flair Designs); metal stencil letters (Scrapworks); square brads (source unknown); cardstock; acrylic paint

## A Boy and His Snake

When Debbie's son brought home a corn snake, she never expected she would eventually become attached to the hissing houseguest. Upon moving, they had to find Coils a new home, but Debbie made this page to reflect upon his beautiful colors, as well as to recall the fond memories the family and Coils shared. The colorful dot patterned paper was a clever way to mimic the look of scales, while machine-stitching enhanced the look of the layout as well. Image-editing software was used to change only the photo backgrounds to black-and-white to keep the focus on Coils.

Debbie Hill, Westford, Massachusetts

**Supplies:** Patterned paper, monogram letter (Basic Grey); image-editing software (Adobe Photoshop); letter tiles, twill snaps (Junkitz); ribbon (Offray); rub-on letters (Junkitz, Making Memories); alcohol inks (Ranger)

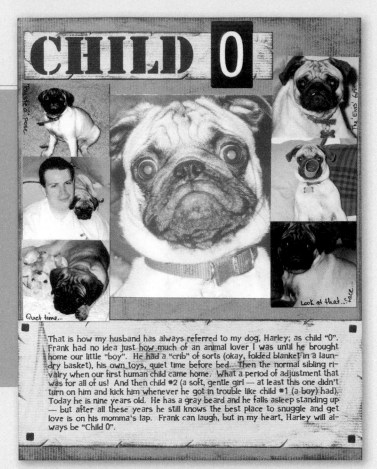

# Child 0

Shay's maternal instincts kicked in full-force the day her husband brought home their child "0," Harley, as she swaddled him, babied him and fussed over him—great practice for human children numbers 1 and 2! Shay used cropped square images of this first baby in their family, creating strips along either side of the central photo to incorporate many of Harley's expressions and antics. By inking her textured cardstocks reminiscent of the hues in Harley's coat, Shay added instant texture and played up his folds and wrinkles.

Shay Brackney, Castle Rock, Colorado

**Supplies:** Textured cardstocks (Bazzill); square brads, mailbox letter (Making Memories); distress ink (Ranger)

# Daisy 2004

A paw in hand is a true sign of trust from a dog, and an even rarer gift coming from a rescue dog. Cheryl's husband has always been supportive of her rescue efforts, and he took this photo of Daisy giving Cheryl her paw to capture the great reward of friendship. Cheryl kept the page design simple, embellishing it with pet-themed items to lend three-dimensional charm and visual interest.

Cheryl Baase, Lansing, Michigan
Photo: Michael Baase, Lansing, Michigan

**Supplies:** Patterned papers, tags (Chatterbox); textured cardstock (Bazzill); pet-themed resin round (Karen Foster Design); rub-on numbers (source unknown); leather paw prints, bone and collar with charms (EK Success); stamping ink

### Dewey & Daniel

A dog and his boy, a boy and his dog—Michelle's son and his dog, Dewey, are an inseparable pair. She represented this closeness in the details of her design by adding a row of ribbon ties beside their photo and with a buckled band stretched below it. She used flattened bottle caps to showcase letter stickers in her title for all-boy appeal and brushed a creamy tan paint and black ink throughout the page for a camouflage effect. Machine-stitching adds a heartwarming touch to this page celebrating treasured, timeless friendship.

Michelle Tornay, Newark, California

**Supplies:** Patterned paper, paper letter tiles, bottle caps (Mustard Moon); ribbons (May Arts, Offray); letter stickers (Me & My Big Ideas); mailbox letters (Making Memories); buckle (Li'l Davis Designs); cardstock; stamping ink; acrylic paint

Daniel, how could I have known how much you would fall in love with Dewey. A dog and his boy, or is it a boy and his dog? I am never quite sure which one it is with the two of you as one minute Dewey is chasing you and the next you are chasing Dewey. I love to watch the two of you together. Daddy and I have affectionately dubbed you trouble A and trouble B and we know that wherever one is the other is close by.

## Man's Best Friend

Chad grew up in a house full of boys, so when his adoring companion, Phoebe, came into his life, she helped him prepare for living with girls by serving as Holly and Chad's first of three. Phoebe's tribute page was computer-generated, allowing for a seamless blend of photos using a feathering technique. To add thematic fun and contrast to the layout, Holly added stock photos of dog bones to meld with the journaling background.

Holly Vandyne, Mansfield, Ohio

**Supplies:** Image-editing software (Adobe Photoshop); stock photo image (iStockPhoto)

## Love•a•ble...

Good Friday grew even better for Ashley when she received her own personal Easter bunny as a special gift. Tammy layered patterned papers on this page celebrating the newfound love between Ashley and Dash, and adhered a printed transparency over the top to sum up just the right sentiments. A funky heart punch design was used to create a frame for the accent photo in the upper right, which was distressed with colored chalks. Tammy's journaling pulls out with a file tab from behind the large photo.

**Tammy Vangen, Marion, Iowa**

**Supplies:** Patterned paper, tags (SEI); textured cardstocks (Bazzill); printed transparency (Creative Imaginations); mini brads (Boxer Scrapbook Productions); heart punch (Emagination Crafts); photo turns (Junkitz); chalk

Ashley's new love - Dash. Dash was Ashley's Easter gift this year. As an animal loving teenager - Ashley has wanted a bunny for quite sometime. On Good Friday 2005, Ashley and I stopped at a pet store in Iowa City and there he was - it was love at first sight! He has spots that are shaped like black hearts around each of his eyes. It was evident right from the start, that Dash was special! He was not at all afraid of Reggie - now he and Reggie have races around the coffee table and through the living room. He loves Ashley, he gives her kisses, when she makes a kiss sound Ashley adores Dash and he adores Ashley! ♡♡♡

With training, **rabbits** can **learn** the meaning of "**no**" and can **respond to their names.** Some can be taught other voice commands such as "**give me a kiss**" or "**go to your cage.**"

## Walk Beside Me...

Although adorable little Rex has sadly left Sally's family since these photos were taken, she knows her son, Carter, is better for having known him, and made this layout as a tribute to their friendship. Sally chose patterned papers using her son's shirt as inspiration, and then inked the edges of the papers and photos to complement the color of Rex's fur. Metal hinges, decorative eyelets and brads add a touch of masculinity, offset by a stencil tag with a soft and heartwarming ribbon.

**Sally Davidson, Kerrville, Texas**

**Supplies:** Patterned papers, rub-on letters (Imagination Project); brads, hinges, swirl eyelets (Making Memories); stencil tag (Autumn Leaves); ribbon; mini jewelry tags; stamping ink

## M & R

Melanie has snapped over 1500 shots of Rocky, who absolutely adores having his picture taken! The secrets behind the seven-year friendship Melanie shares with her pug are tucked behind the pair's photo on a beautifully distressed journaling tag. Melanie used close-up photos of Rocky's facial features, taken at his level, and angled them on the left of this loving layout. A ribbon along the bottom embellished with a decorative clip lends the look of a collar to the design, while square conchos set in several of the photos provide the perfect captions.

Melanie St-Cyr, Lachine, Quebec, Canada

**Supplies:** Patterned paper (7 Gypsies, Daisy D's); textured cardstock (Bazzill); decorative foam corner, foam letter stamps (Making Memories); rub-on letters (Autumn Leaves); square frame conchos, square paper clip (Scrapworks); ribbons; staples; pen; stamping ink

## Forever Love...
## Cody and Katy

The tender love shared between two babies is expressed in the photo of Jenn's son, Cody, sweetly kissing his new puppy's little nose. Jenn set up this photo shoot on her porch, using an ironing board covered with a tablecloth to create the photo background. The page itself was designed on the computer using layers of papers, ribbon and transparencies from a digital kit.

Jenn Brookover, San Antonio, Texas

**Supplies:** Image-editing software (Adobe Photoshop Elements 2.0); patterned papers, transparencies, brushes, stamps, ribbon (Rhonna Farrer, www.twopeasin abucket.com)

It has been **scientifically proven** that **stroking a pet** can **reduce** a person's **blood pressure**.

## Then & Now

The fascination between boys and frogs spans the test of time. In this generational layout, Julie combined a photo of her husband as a young boy holding an amphibian friend with a similar image of their own boys. She designed her own frog-themed paper with her word processor and downloaded frog postage stamps from the Internet. Julie created a striking effect by converting her photos to black-and-white using photo-editing software, with only the green of the frogs remaining for emphasis.

Julie McCauley, Hesperia, California
**Photos:** James McCauley Sr., James McCauley, Hesperia, California

**Supplies:** Patterned paper (made using Microsoft Works); metal frame, brads (Jo-Ann Stores); letter, magnetic letter and date stamps (Making Memories); ribbon (Michaels); frog charm (source unknown); colored staples (Target); textured cardstock; transparency; stamping inks; frog postage stamps (downloaded from Internet); image-editing software (Adobe Photoshop Elements 2.0); acrylic paint

ADORE

Faithful Friends

LOVE

Tyler

Pip

xoxo

There is no love like the love between a boy & his dog.
-unknown

Now that Pip is over a year old and mostly out of his puppy stage, Tyler & Pip have a great friendship. They had a good one before but Pip does a better job listening to Tyler now which makes it so much easier! Pip still has his "I am not listening" moments though. Pip will follow Tyler around watching what he is doing & playing with. Could be that Pip is just waiting for Tyler to drop a toy so he can run off with it but. Pip is getting better about that too. Outside they run & play together and Tyler will blow bubbles for Pip to chase after. They fight over couch space and the blanket but then end up falling asleep together. Most of the time Pip just wants a warm lap to curl up in and usually it is Tyler who is watching TV at the right time. Tyler calls Pip his "little brother" and just like brothers they fight too. Most of the time it is because Pip is getting into Tyler's toys, running off with one of his stuffed bears or even ruining his one of his forts. But overall they get along really well, are great friends and love each other very much.

## Faithful Friends

Designing a layout around the ever-changing relationship between Miki's son, Tyler, and his dog, Pip, was a great way to use up a large number of random photos she had of the two together. Several black-and-white photos of Tyler and Pip over the years complement the soft, yet masculine, look of the page, embellished with stitching and stapled ribbons. Miki used monograms, letter stickers, cut patterned papers and more to decorate the front of the file folder, which opens to reveal a warm color photo and journaling describing the unique friendship between this boy and his dog.

**Miki Benedict, Modesto, California**

**Supplies:** Patterned papers, monogram letters (FontWerks); textured cardstock (Bazzill); letter stickers (American Crafts); "Faithful Friends" sticker (Bo-Bunny Press); love-themed label stickers (Pebbles); heart charm, staples (Making Memories); mini brad (Boxer Scrapbook Productions); ribbons; vellum; thread

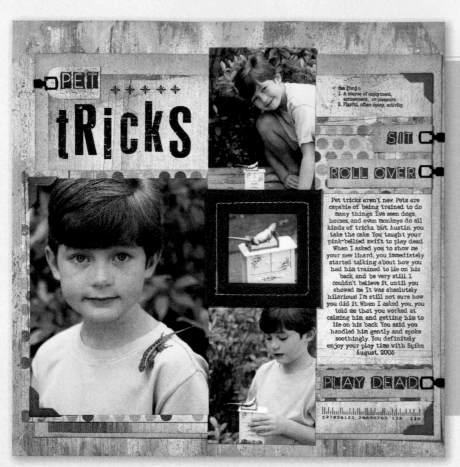

## Pet Tricks

There are many pets that can do amazing tricks, but Angelia was floored when Austin showed her the ways he had trained his pink-bellied swift to sit, roll over and even play dead! She created this layout to feature Spike in action and shots of Austin coaching his trickster lizard. Layered blue, green and gray papers add playful, boyish charm to the page. A stitched leather frame completes the look, drawing attention to Spike playing dead, as well as adding a touch of lizardlike texture.

Angelia Wigginton, Belmont, Mississippi

**Supplies:** Patterned papers (Basic Grey, Bo-Bunny Press); rub-on letters, photo corners, clips (Heidi Swapp); stitched leather frame (Li'l Davis Designs); rub-on definition word (Rusty Pickle); rub-on flower (Autumn Leaves); stamping ink

## Love That Cat

A black cardstock backdrop adds drama to Heide's largely pastel layout featuring black-and-white images of her cat and a color-centric quote that inspired her design. The simple wording launches this dynamic layout into a modern-edged design, featuring soft colors against clear-cut lines and curves. Heide created her own paper embellishments by using basic-punch shapes to create the striking, graphic look.

Heide Lasher, Englewood, Colorado

**Supplies:** Textured cardstock (Bazzill); circle punch (EK Success); square punch (Marvy); cardstock

Some **notable people who adored cats:**
**Abraham Lincoln, Winston Churchill, Florence Nightingale, Mark Twain, Buddha, Muhammed, Ernest Hemingway** and **Henry David Thoreau.**

With dogs and people,
it's love in
big splashy colors.
When you're
involved with a cat,
you're dealing
with pastels.

Louis J. Camuti

love
.............that cat

## Sophie

### & Finny

Finny & Sophia, Sophie & Finney – Usually where you find one you will find the other.

We have quite a few pets in our home. We like to refer to it as our little menagerie. We have two golden retrievers and four, yes that's 4, cats.

For some odd reason thought, Finnegan and Sophie seem to have bonded more so than any other pet.

His appearance is deceiving. When you first take a look at his greying face and stern exterior, most people think is the old man of the family when, in reality, he is the youngest of all the animals we have. It just turned out that he was one of those "men" that turned grey prematurely. Go figure!

Our baby boy started life out as the runt of the litter. Our decision to adopt him came because of our long work hours in the city and our feeling that Sydney (our oldest Golden Retriever) would be lonely by herself all day in house until we arrived home.

We saw his eager little face in the litter and he was so small and inactive compared to his brothers and sisters. They seemed to walk all over him and he just sat there. That was all it took and he came home with us that very day.

The ironic thing about him just sitting in his pen while the puppies trampled him, is that, the very same trait has enabled him to put up with an active toddler who does the same things to him.

Sophie would jump on him and pull his ears and just play with his tail and he would just sit there quietly and take all the abuse she would just dish out. We immediately knew that the two of them would be lifelong friends.

Finny has turned out to be her protector, playmate and all around mush ball.

PLAY MATES

### Finny & Sophie

Finny's kind, patient spirit is showcased on Amy's two-page spread, which features tender moments caught on film and vibrant, refreshing colors. Amy kept the look of the pages simple, using the left page to focus solely on the chummy photo, which is highlighted by a dog collar element created using printed twill, snap latches and a circle-cropped photo for the look of a tag. For the right page, Amy printed her journaling directly onto the cardstock and accented each photo with acrylic word embellishments. A band of rub-on words ties the two pages together.

Amy Goldstein, Kent Lakes, New York

**Supplies:** Patterned paper (Scenic Route Paper Co.); textured cardstock (Bazzill); rub-on words (Making Memories); printed twill, snap latches, acrylic words (Junkitz)

# Ideas for Custom Pet Page Additions

• **Mimic the look of rawhide and dog biscuits by creating clay page accents using either air-dry or baking clay.**
Simply roll out the clay to approximately ⅛" thickness, use templates or cookie cutters to create the shapes, then bake as directed or let dry for 24 hours. Add color with acrylic paint and rub-ons.

• **Create an imprint of your pet's paw using paper clay.** Roll out the clay to approximately ⅛" and gently press your pet's paw into the clay. Trim away excess. Let air dry 24 hours and add color to enhance definition.

• **Have small pets walk across a pigment inkpad, then immediately onto nearby paper for the look of tiny pet tracks.**

• **Engrave blank pet identification tags available at pet supply stores for dimensional page additions.**

• **Create your own patterned paper by repeating fun phrases or your pet's name across the page and then print onto desired paper.**

# Teacher's Pet

From home school mascot to head of the class, Ginger the pup worked her way up to the status of Teacher's Pet. This colorful page design exudes thematic charm, with a composition notebook cover adorned with vivid ribbons and fibers. Deb even included Ginger's paw print on the layout, stamping her paw in green paint, onto paper and then onto the black cardstock, stapling the cut-out image to twine. Deb used computer-editing software to create her own filmstrip element as well.

Deb Perry, Newport News, Virginia

**Supplies:** Patterned paper (Paper Fever, Treehouse Designs); textured cardstock (Bazzill); ribbons, fibers (May Arts, Michaels); letter stickers (Bo-Bunny Press, Creative Memories, Sticker Studio); license plate sticker (Sticker Studio); acrylic frame (Making Memories); image-editing software (Adobe Photoshop); transparency; acrylic paint; staples; composition notebook; twine; pop tab; pen

# Dogs...Make Our Lives Whole

Upon returning from a business trip, Mary was greeted by the adoring face of a new family member, Howie. Immediately Mary began taking photos of Howie and her husband together to document the special bond that had already begun. The green, distressed-effect patterned paper set the perfect background for the black-and-white photos, and played up the textures of the inseparable duo in the grass. Mary inked and painted the borders of the layered papers to coordinate with the patterned paper, and then used rivets, staples and a washer word for masculine flair.

Mary MacAskill, Calgary, Alberta, Canada

**Supplies:** Patterned papers (Doodlebug Design, Paper Loft), textured cardstock (Bazzill); stencil letter (Autumn Leaves); photo corner, washer word (Making Memories); rivets (K & Company); label maker (Dymo); stamping ink; acrylic paint; twine; staples; transparency

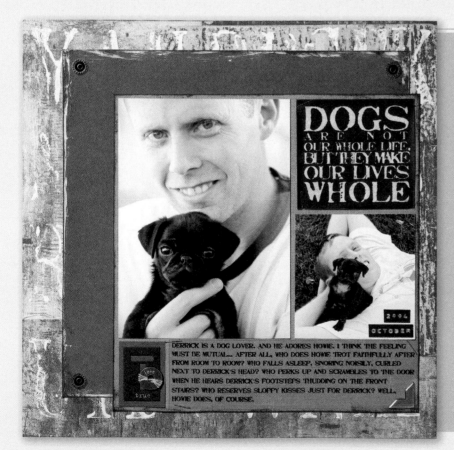

a dog's life

Every day when we come home from work, we know that we will be greeted by two of the friendliest, lovable faces one could ever hope for. No matter what kind of day you have, good or bad, you can always count on our little boobahs (our endearing name for them) to put a smile on your face simply by their greetings alone.

I'M HOME!! I come in the door and right away, Indy is walking along side me on the top of the couch and jumps down to greet me and give me plenty of kisses. Afterwards, Chewie also greets me with her loving kisses and then proceeds to run to her toys and grab her favorite, rope dog, and roll on top of him. I'm not too sure why she does this, but it makes me smile. I feel like it's a special thing that she likes to show me because she knows I am home to see it.

DADDY'S HOME!! When Dan comes home, it's a little different, but they greet him with wagging tails and warm kisses, just the same. Chewie gets so excited that she first has to have her tummy rubbed and then she runs back and forth like a little lightning bolt around Dan and around the house. Indy gets equally as thrilled and he becomes Dan's little shadow. The minute Dan gets home, you can bet Indy will be by his side no matter where he goes.

It's great to be loved!!

WAITING for mom and DAD

Indy          CHEWie

WATCHDOG

## Waiting for Mom and Dad

Janetta knows firsthand how wonderful it is to be loved, which she illustrates in this layout depicting her two dogs waiting with baited breath to see their "mom and dad." Her journaling shares her dogs' daily routine and welcome-home performance specifically tailored to each owner's return. A mix of browns and creams provide warmth and complement the black-and-white photos, while paw print twill sticker strips and patterned paper add an element of fun.

Janetta Abucejo Wieneke, Memory Makers Books

**Supplies:** Patterned papers (Around The Block, Sticker Studio); paw print sticker strips, watch dog sticker (Flair Designs); rub-on dog phrase, leash (American Traditional Designs); rub-on letters (Imagination Project); word stickers (Magnetic Poetry)

**Dogs** have shown the ability **to detect seizures** prior to their occurrence, the **presence of autism** in children and even certain forms of **cancer.**

# Friends

A tender moment shared between these two friends was a thrill for Karen to capture on film. She set these black-and-white images of bonding between her child and dog against festive, playful colors and pet-themed stickers and accents. Soft velvet ribbon coordinates with the red acrylic heart and heart tag as well, spreading the look of love around the page.

Karen Day for Flair Designs, Little Rock, Arkansas

**Supplies:** Patterned paper, pet-themed stickers, velvet ribbon (Flair Designs); textured cardstock (Bazzill); heart tag, letter stickers (Doodlebug Design); mini brads (Lasting Impressions); rub-on letters (Making Memories); acrylic heart (Heidi Grace Designs); ribbon (Offray)

What a sweet moment when I looked over to see Holly and Jackson laying on the floor together. It didn't surprise me at all to find them together, because Jackson loves with a heart that is really 10 sizes too big. Everything he loves knows that love, actually it is smothered in that love.

On this afternoon, Holly was the lucky one to get the love, and I was even luckier to catch it on film. But there is so much that the pictures don't tell. They can't recount the unintelligible conversation that Jackson was having or the sweet tone of his voice. Those are locked away in my heart and mind for me to retell fir years to come.

Jackson and Holly
February 2004

A **dog** named **Laikia** became the **world's first astronaut** in 1957 when she was sent into space by the **Russian government**.

# L

Sweet sophistication is expressed in Jill's page, which depicts the special love she shares with her dog, Lilly. Jill created the pretty, preppy look of the page by designing her own "patterned paper" using foam stamps and ink. Pairs of eyelets in the upper portion of the page are laced with perky ribbons for a festive touch, while a monogram letter stamp balances off the minimal journaling block at the bottom.

Jill Barnett, Goose Creek, South Carolina
Photos: Trevor Barnett, Goose Creek, South Carolina

**Supplies:** Textured cardstock (Bazzill); foam diamond stamps (Heidi Swapp); foam letter stamp (Making Memories); diamond and circle stamps (Font-Werks); ribbons (American Crafts); chalk inks (Clearsnap); eyelets; pen

Waiting to get a dog paid off in a big way! Lilly is so awesome & loving that I can't imagine any other pet. Everyday, she nuzzles & kisses me, bringing smiles to my face. –July 2005

# Reptile

Shannon's son, Robby, was tickled green to be the proud new owner of a pet snake—if only for a few days. Shannon created this layout to commemorate the smile on Robby's face and the joy that he found in his slithering sidekick. She used polka-dot foam stamps across green patterned paper to create the look of scales, as well as on the button embellishments on either side of the title made to look like eyes. For a fun and dimensional extra touch, Shannon added jump rings to accentuate randomly stamped dots about the page.

Shannon Taylor, Bristol, Tennessee

**Supplies:** Patterned paper, jump rings (Junkitz); clear title letters, dot foam stamp (Heidi Swapp); button embellishments (Magic Scraps); number stamps (Hero Arts); dimensional adhesive (JudiKins); metal plaque, reptile textured paper (source unknown); mini brads; acrylic paint

DREAMS COME TRUE

2004

A dream come true for Robby...a nightmare for his mother. Papaw Bob brought a snake from his farm just for Robby. And for a short few days, it was love. Robby called it grassy green named for a snake his daddy had in childhood. Despite my objections, he held it consistently.... IN THE HOUSE! They were buddies, compadres, soul mates, but the fun didn't last. Turns out it was a girl & was getting ready to lay an egg. It didn't want to be touched any more. Robby was completely bummed out! So we had to let it go back to the farm. But for just a few days, Robby had his very own pet snake and was completely happy.
-2004

## Bubbles Beware

Heather's son, Trent, had a day of sheer joy discovering his dog's absolute love (or hatred) of bubbles! Circle patterned strips define the boundaries of Heather's design and carry the look of the bubbles across the layout. A few strategically placed acrylic embellishments give this bouncy page effervescent charm, while highlighting select letters and circle print elements.

Heather Binnie, Tucson, Arizona

**Supplies:** Patterned papers (Carolee's Creations, Chatterbox, Rusty Pickle); textured cardstock (Bazzill); rub-on letters (Chart-Pak, Li'l Davis Designs); acrylic accents (Heidi Grace Designs); letter stamps (PSX Design); stamping inks; pen

> Pets enhance positive self-esteem and **loving, nurturing behavior** in children, who in turn are likely **to grow into compassionate adults.**

## A Dog and His Boy

Almost like siblings, but more like best friends, Michelle's son, Daniel, and his dog, Dewey, are perfect playmates. Michelle's page features black-and-white images of these kindred spirits, bound by a measuring tape to celebrate their growing up together. A bottle cap accent lends subtle masculine flair, while inked edges capture the rough-and-tumble feeling of "brothers" at play. Michelle used large letter stickers to emphasize key words in her prominent title, establishing balance on the page.

**Michelle Tornay**, Newark, California

**Supplies:** Patterned paper, bottle cap, paper letter tiles (Mustard Moon); textured cardstock (Bazzill); ribbons (Offray); measuring tape (Jo-Ann Stores); letter stickers (American Crafts); rub-on letters (EK Success); stamping ink

## My Girls

Pam's husband captured this snuggling session between Pam and her two sweet girls. The name tabs on either side of this tender trio pull out to reveal the personality traits and special places each of these "daughters" hold in the hearts of their family. Burgundy silk flowers set against rust-colored cardstock draw out the warm colors from the photo, while quiet green elements complement the look. A variety of stitches, a decorative photo corner and ribbons establish a timeless look of love.

**Pam Callaghan**, Bowling Green, Ohio
**Photo:** Kevin Callaghan, Bowling Green, Ohio

**Supplies:** Patterned paper (Basic Grey); textured cardstocks (Bazzill); ribbon (Making Memories, Offray); small metal-rimmed tag, photo corner (EK Success); decorative brad (Making Memories); circle frame (Karen Foster Design); rub-on letters (Imagination Project); silk flowers; staples; transparency; stamping ink

*Missy*

Missy has been my dog for almost 8 years. She has been an amazing companion whenever I have needed her. Kevin calls her "my dog" because she follows me around everywhere. Missy is the ultimate protector, as she would defend any family member if needed. Her bark is mean, but behind the bark, lies the sweetest German Shepherd I know.

*Daphne*

Daphne is only a few months old. From as long as I can remember, I have wanted a great big dog! When we picked out Daphne, we never imagined that she would be a true "gentle giant." She is not only my dog, she is everyone's dog. Daphne is incredible with Sean, she is growing up right beside him and treats him as a playmate yet respects his authority over him. I look forward to seeing Daphne grow up with Sean.

## P&B 1977

Some friendships you never forget, as is evident between these two childhood companions in a photo taken when Paula was just 6 years old. She created this page to incorporate a layout about herself into a scrapbook she made for her son, sharing the fond memories of her furry confidant. Paula established a soft and feminine, yet funky and fun, tone to the page using playful patterns in quiet colors, with an emphasis on pink accents. A wire flower set at the bottom of her photo adds a sense of whimsy.

Paula Gerhart, Valencia, California

Photo: Dennis Walman, Palmdale, California

**Supplies:** Patterned paper, cardstocks, cardstock number stickers (SEI); dog quote sticker (Wordsworth); rub-on letters, metal-rimmed tags (Making Memories); metal flower accent (source unknown); brad; staples; stamping ink; acrylic paints

## A World of Wonder

The wonder of a child is a beautiful thing, as Cheryl proves with these photos of her daughter's fascination with her fish, Ruby Ann. Cheryl loved the vivid colors of the patterned papers she chose for this page that coordinate with the fishbowl décor, and festive fibers convey a free-flowing look similar to the aquatic plants. Cheryl completed the look of the layout by adding clear micro beads throughout to mimic the look of bubbles.

Cheryl Waters, Laguna Niguel, California

**Supplies:** Patterned papers, letter stickers, monogram, fibers (Basic Grey); textured cardstock (Bazzill); decorative paper (handmade, Magenta); tag (2Dye4); ribbons; transparency; beads; eyelet; foam adhesive spacers

# Friendship

The friendship enjoyed between Ruth's daughter, Rachel, and their English bulldog, Bentley, grows richer every day. Ruth designed this soft and sweet page to cherish the ways the two are growing up together, and used a silk flower for sentiment and to symbolize their blossoming friendship. Black, stitched ribbon was used to create strong borders around the photo corners and to display the definition sticker in an eye-pleasing way.

Ruth Halford, Conway, South Carolina

**Supplies:** Patterned paper (K & Company); textured cardstock (Bazzill); clear definition sticker, mini brads, ribbon (Making Memories); photo turns, clear button (7 Gypsies); silk flower; hemp string

# Buddies

Ready to take on the world, this dynamic duo can be found most any given day as an inseparable force in Linda's backyard. Linda based her design around the shapes and colors of a metro sign for a masculine yet playful look and feel. She used a paw print punch on the lower portion of the orange element for contrast against the light gray background and added the punched-out portion for balance in the lower left.

Linda Harrison, Sarasota, Florida

**Supplies:** Patterned paper (source unknown); textured cardstocks (Bazzill); rub-on letters (Making Memories); circle punch (Punch Bunch); paw print punch (Marvy)

## I Will Never Stop Loving You

The love Jill has in her heart for her SkippyBear will always live on in her heart and on this tender memorial page. She used warm, sunny colors and flowers to accentuate her beloved companion's marmalade fur and sweet disposition. The bottom right photo of the two friends opens to reveal a single photo of SkippyBear, as well as journaling that shares Jill's sorrow over losing such a faithful companion. Ribbons tied to the top of her layout add textural finesse while a combination of round metal letters, painted wooden and metal letters create a visually appealing title and heartfelt tribute.

Jill Cornelius, Allen, Texas

**Supplies:** Patterned paper (Chatterbox); textured cardstock (Bazzill); metal letters, ribbons (Making Memories); wooden letters (Li'l Davis Designs); silk flowers; acrylic paint

You were my faithful friend for over twelve years. You were there for the good times and the bad. But when you needed me I wasn't there. I feel terribly guilty for not being there when you needed me. I feel that if I had stayed home and had not gone on vacation that you would still be here with me, cuddling on the couch or laying in bed and watching TV with me. I will never be able to pet you again, look into your eyes and see your happiness or hear your sweet meow. I will always remember the times that you would jump on the chair behind me, or stand in front of me and just look at me. I will remember when you and I were all alone. When we went through the rough times and when we had happy times also. I will remember the nicknames that I had given you, fluffybutt, Skippybear, Skippycat. I am sure that there are others but the sadness in my heart is so strong that I can't bear to think of them since it would bring tears that I know won't end. I miss you so much, and I don't think that anyone could really understand or would understand why. How can you miss an animal, a pet. Well, it's simple. You were not a pet, you were my friend, my best furry friend. I know I will have to go on without you beside me, but you and your love will always live on in my heart and in my memories. I will miss you my little Skippybear.

It has been estimated that **people who own pets live longer,** have **less stress,** experience **less depression** and have **fewer heart attacks.**

## Beware Cute Dog

Whether Wendy's son is playing video games, watching TV or running around outside, his lovable pal Dawson is always at his feet. Wendy's layout conveys an all-boy attitude to showcase the special bond between these two pals. She tilted the photo to line up with the slanted images on her patterned paper and sanded and inked the blue background paper to meld with the overall feel of the page. For a final touch of pet-themed fun, a ball chain is suspended across the page and is enhanced by cardstock dog tags.

**Wendy Malichio, Bethel, Connecticut**

**Supplies:** Patterned paper, cardstock tags, letters, twill fabric stickers (Paper House Productions); clips (7 Gypsies); ball chain, photo turns (Making Memories); stamping ink

## These Are a Few of My Favorite Things

Copper the kitty is Michon's daughter's absolute favorite thing, and with beautiful flowers in the background of her photos, Michon incorporated some of her favorite things as well. For a dreamy addition to her file folder accent, Michon scanned a photo of Copper onto a transparency, cut out blocks from the folder and set the transparency behind it to reveal his furry facial features. The journaling inside shares details of this cat and this little girl's special bond.

**Michon Kessler, Alturas, California**

**Supplies:** Patterned paper (Colorbök, Diane's Daughters, Karen Foster Design); textured paper, brads, file folder, window frame-making set (Provo Craft); ribbon (Offray); pet-themed stickers (Karen Foster Design); distress ink (Ranger); acrylic paint

This is one of my favorite photos of you Makayla. You fell sooooo head over heals in love with this little kitten. Daddy took you and your sisters out to Hamel's Ranch and picked out two little scrawny kittens. Copper is the only one that survived unfortunately. They were both very sick little kitties when you guys brought them home. You love this cat more than anything right now. You treat him just like you would your own little baby and he lets you!

Picture taken March 2004

**CH PENDRAGON'S MARVELOUS MERLIN 1994 - 2005**

Common ways that **pet owners express their love** for their animals are by **celebrating their** pets' **birthdays**, buying them **holiday gifts, displaying their photos** in their homes and fixing them **special treats and meals.**

## CH Pendragon's Marvelous Merlin

Kimberley's memorial page to the family's beloved mastiff, Merlin, is a reminder to cherish every moment shared with our canine friends, just as they do with us. The large, close-up photo of Merlin captures the gentleness in his eyes and the important role he played in his family, with his registered name and lifespan listed beneath. The right page shows his loving family by his side, even through his last moments, with journaling that highlights the special ways he brought so much happiness into their lives.

**Kimberley Wall, Grand Rapids, Michigan**

**Supplies:** Patterned paper (EK Success); textured cardstock (Bazzill); stamping ink

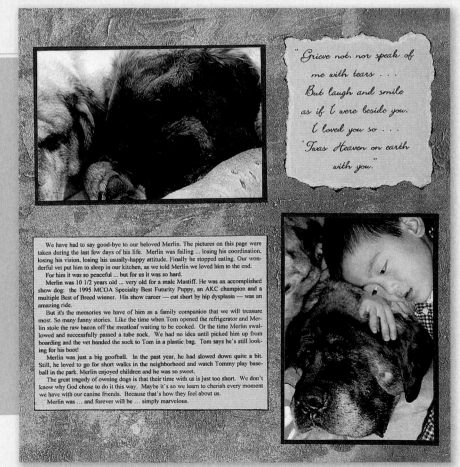

" Grieve not, nor speak of me with tears . . . But laugh and smile as if I were beside you. I loved you so . . . 'Twas Heaven on earth with you."

We have had to say good-bye to our beloved Merlin. The pictures on this page were taken during the last few days of his life. Merlin was failing ... losing his coordination, losing his vision, losing his usually-happy attitude. Finally he stopped eating. Our wonderful vet put him to sleep in our kitchen, as we told Merlin we loved him to the end. For him it was so peaceful ... but for us it was so hard.

Merlin was 10 1/2 years old ... very old for a male Mastiff. He was an accomplished show dog: the 1995 MCOA Specialty Best Futurity Puppy, an AKC champion and a multiple Best of Breed winner. His show career — cut short by hip dysplasia — was an amazing ride.

But it's the memories we have of him as a family companion that we will treasure most. So many funny stories. Like the time when Tom opened the refrigerator and Merlin stole the raw bacon off the meatloaf waiting to be cooked. Or the time Merlin swallowed and successfully passed a tube sock. We had no idea until picked him up from boarding and the vet handed the sock to Tom in a plastic bag. Tom says he's still looking for his boot!

Merlin was just a big goofball. In the past year, he had slowed down quite a bit. Still, he loved to go for short walks in the neighborhood and watch Tommy play baseball in the park. Merlin enjoyed children and he was so sweet.

The great tragedy of owning dogs is that their time with us is just too short. We don't know why God chose to do it this way. Maybe it's so we learn to cherish every moment we have with our canine friends. Because that's how they feel about us.

Merlin was ... and forever will be ... simply marvelous.

## Angel Hair Puppy

The silky sheen of Kona's fur glows in these photos and in the hearts and fond memories of his family. Trisha created this page as a tribute to her late and much-beloved four-legged "son," and included soft strands of his hair in a clear vinyl pocket. She sealed the pocket closed by creating a folio closure with two distressed punched hearts, brads and floss. To tuck away her heartfelt sentiments, Trisha affixed a manila folder to the back of the layout, and then created a tablike pull-out from an 8½ x 11" sheet of black paper to which she adhered her journaling. A ribbon and charm were used to create a crestlike pull tab adornment.

Trisha McCarty-Luedke, Denver, Colorado

**Supplies:** Patterned paper (Me & My Big Ideas, Scenic Route Paper Co.); rub-on crest, monogram (Melissa Frances); rub-on sentiment, definition sticker (Making Memories); ribbon (Jo-Ann Stores); metal charm (K & Company); die-cut letter (QuicKutz); heart punch (Punch Bunch); cardstock; brads; vinyl; embroidery floss; manila folder; stamping ink

# Remembering Beloved Pets

**Saying goodbye to a cherished pet is never easy, but preserving your precious memories in scrapbooks will help keep your happy memories alive. Here are some ideas for paying tribute to the special love and companionship you shared with your pet.**

• **Devote an entire album to your pet's life.** Showcase your photos and memorabilia in chronological order and incorporate treasured memorabilia, actual or reproduction.

• **Dedicate honorary pages in your family album to your pet** to celebrate the ways your pet enriched your household.

• **Include the contributions of others who loved your pet.** Enclose sympathy cards, e-mails and loving sentiments provided by friends and family members. Some may even wish to design their own pages to add to your albums, or may offer to pen a touching tribute to tuck inside a page pocket. Young children may find comfort in expressing their feelings in drawings and special messages of their own.

• **Journal from your heart.** These pages represent the story of your pet's life and the wonderful bond you shared. Don't leave anything out. Recall your happiest times over the years so that the joy your pet added to your life may be felt and remembered each and every time you revisit your pages.

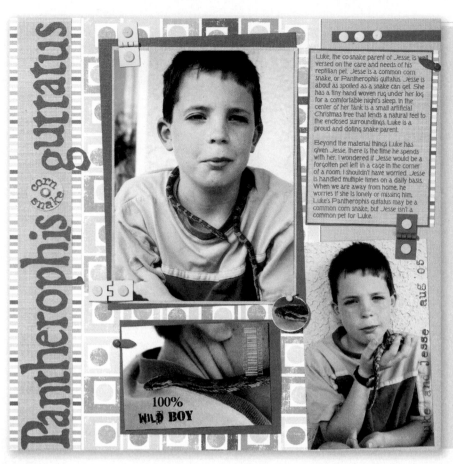

Luke, the co-snake parent of Jesse, is well versed on the care and needs of his reptilian pet. Jesse is a common corn snake, or Pantherophis guttatus. Jesse is about as spoiled as a snake can get. She has a tiny hand woven rug under her log for a comfortable night's sleep. In the center of her tank is a small artificial Christmas tree that lends a natural feel to the enclosed surroundings. Luke is a proud and doting snake parent.

Beyond the material things Luke has given Jesse, there is the time he spends with her. I wondered if Jesse would be a forgotten pet left in a cage in the corner of a room. I shouldn't have worried. Jesse is handled multiple times on a daily basis. When we are away from home, he worries if she is lonely or missing him. Luke's Pantherophis guttatus may be a common corn snake, but Jesse isn't a common pet for Luke.

100% WILD BOY

luke and jesse aug 05

# Pantherophis Guttatus

Jesse the corn snake is an uncommon pet and much-loved friend to Luke, and these photos were taken to show the ways these two "wild things" interact. The handcut title reflects the proper scientific name for Jesse, while Luke's devotion to his coiled comrade is revealed in the journaling passage. Michelle chose energetic colors and patterns for this layout to convey the energy of her preteen son. She tilted the mats and photos for a slightly haphazard look and cropped a close-up of Jesse with a circle punch that she set on a chipboard round.

Michelle Pendleton, Surprise, Arizona

**Supplies:** Patterned paper (Chatterbox, Scenic Route Paper Co.); textured cardstock, chipboard circles (Bazzill); colored brads, hinges, photo clips, snaps (Making Memories); letter and number stamps, circle punch (EK Success); word stamps (Technique Tuesday); rub-on bar code (Basic Grey); solvent ink (Tsukineko); chalk ink (Clearsnap)

# Best Buddies

Man's best friendship can be found on Holly's layout, which is dedicated to the bond shared between her husband and their dog, Shiley. Sepia-tone photos combined with brown and black papers give the page a masculine look, while torn edges, corrugated cardstock and wooden accents add additional ruggedness to the design. Holly inked and painted over and around the torn edges to create cohesiveness and to intensify the boys-at-play attitude.

Holly Hafner, Columbus, Georgia

**Supplies:** Patterned paper, tag stickers (Pebbles); eyelets (Making Memories); word sticker (K & Company); cardstock; corrugated paper; acrylic paint; stamping ink; pen

Best Buddies

friend

John & Shiley
Cooper Creek
Summer 2004

# Love

This computer-generated page dedicated to Susan's pint-sized pal was created with the help of a downloadable kit. Punchy colors, numerous patterns and a bold, graphic composition carry the eye easily throughout the page. Complete with all the charms of a traditional scrapbook page, Susan's digital design boasts layered papers, ribbon and letter accents, making for a cheery way to profess her love and affection for her Chihuahua.

Susan Merrell, Starkville, Mississippi

**Supplies:** Image-editing software (Adobe Photoshop 7.0); digital elements (Piece-a-Cake page kit, http://shabbyprincess .com/SweetSprinkles.asp)

# Lauren & Eddie

Lauren loves to snuggle with her feline pal, Eddie, anytime and any place. Robyn caught these two cuddling under a patio table one day and designed this digital layout to express their mutual friendship. All of the cozy page elements were downloaded from a digital scrapbooking kit, except for the brads and ribbon topper which were added separately. The word art set below Lauren's joyful grin sums up the photo perfectly.

Robyn England, Mansfield, Texas

**Supplies:** Image-editing software (Adobe Photoshop CS); patterned paper, stitching, word art and tag (digital scrapbook kit from Rhonna Farrer, www.twopeasinabucket.com); brads, ribbon topper (Cheryl Barber)

## Dog Days of Summer Album Featuring "Summer Treat"

Leah designed the cover of this 6 x 6" album with retro-cool appeal. She handcut and inked the large title letters for a distressed effect and combined them with letter and pet-themed stickers. She also used the stickers (part of a pet-themed kit) as titles and accents on her interior spread, mounting a couple on foam adhesive spacers for dimension. By cropping her photos to be in keeping with the scale of the smaller page format, she created an abundance of space for journaling and creativity.

Leah Blanco Williams,
Rochester, New York

Supplies: Dog Scrapbook kit (Xyron); distress ink (Ranger); foam adhesive spacers; pen

# A Cat's Life Album Featuring "Cat Nap"

Sharon created the cover of this album by cutting the title words from patterned paper and then stitching them for texture, balancing the frenzy of ribbons tied to the spiral-ring spine. To feature the sleeping escapades of Willie the cat in her interior spread, she called upon her sewing machine to create swirling ripples around the borders and over the top layers of patterned paper squares for a ball-of-yarn playfulness. Cat-themed metal charms embellished with ribbons lend additional visual delight.

**Sharon Laakkonen, Superior, Wisconsin**

**Cover Supplies:** Patterned paper, metal frame, cat charm, mini album (American Traditional Designs); ribbons (American Traditional Designs, Making Memories, May Arts, Offray); distress ink (Ranger); mini brads (Queen & Co.); buttons, sewing machine

**Layout Supplies:** Patterned papers, cardstock, metal charms, stickers (American Traditional Designs); mini brads (Queen & Co.); ribbons (American Traditional Designs, Making Memories); distress ink (Ranger)

# Z Album Featuring "What's in a Name"

Kari's album features a fabric photo transfer that was cut with pinking shears and given additional detail with machine-stitching. The image was backed with batting, adorned with buttons and mounted over frayed gingham. Printed twill, a touch of ribbon, buttons and more gingham complete the highly tactile mini book, which opens to reveal a whimsical spread that explains the story behind Zooey's J.D. Salinger-inspired name. Coordinating patterned papers with stitched and slightly roughed edges, a printed transparency, and cut and stitched paper elements mounted on foam adhesive comprise Kari's appealing page backgrounds. Velvet ribbon and a die-cut title provide purr-fect finishing touches to play up Zooey's striking photos.

Kari Hansen, *Memory Makers* magazine

**Cover Supplies:** Corduroy album (C.R. Gibson); inkjet twill fabric (Color Textiles); twill alphabet letter (Carolee's Creations); paw print twill (Creative Impressions); iron-on fabric adhesive (Therm O Web); fabric; ribbon; covered button; pearl buttons; thread; pinking shears; batting

**Layout Supplies:** Textured cardstock (Bazzill); patterned papers, velvet ribbon (Flair Designs); die-cut letters (QuicKutz); transparency; photo paper; thread; foam adhesivetwill alphabet letter (Carolee's Creations); paw print twill (Creative Impressions); iron-on fabric adhesive (Therm O Web); fabric; ribbon; covered button; pearl buttons; thread; pinking shears; batting

# Who Loves You Indy? Album Featuring..."Daddy" and "Mommy"

A visual treat resides on the cover of Janetta's album, created for Indiana, a.k.a "Indy." She placed photo corners on each corner of her dog-themed paper and matted a strip of faux cork paper for her sticker title treatment. An eyelet ribbon along the binding gives the impression of a collar. Inside, the spread assures Indy how much he is loved by his "Daddy" and "Mommy." The left page features Indy with Janetta's husband, Dan, and a handwritten love note from Dan to his furry "son" under a flip-up card. The right page reverses the look of the left. Mini photo squares and dog charms are staggered on the inside borders of each page for a unified spread.

**Janetta Abucejo Wieneke, Memory Makers Books**

**Cover Supplies:** Black corduroy album (C.R.Gibson); patterned papers, letter stickers, epoxy stickers, decorative license plate, dog-themed stickers (Karen Foster Design); textured cardstock (Bazzill); eyelet ribbon (Junkitz); die-cut photo corners (Sizzix); question mark sticker (Creative Imaginations)

**Layout Supplies:** Patterned papers, fire hydrant charm, dog bowl charm, furry friend charm, dog collar charm, brads (Karen Foster Design); textured cardstock (Bazzill); stamped expressions (Stamping Sensations); dog brads (Around The Block); die-cut photo corner (Sizzix); chalk ink (Clearsnap); stamping ink; foam adhesive spacers

# Pet Quotes of Note

## Dogs

The reason a dog has so many friends is that he wags his tail instead of his tongue.—Unknown

Happiness is a warm puppy.—Charles Schultz

No matter how little money and how few possessions you own, having a dog makes you rich.—Louis Sabin

Money will buy you a pretty good dog, but it won't buy you the wag of his tail.—Josh Billings

The greatest pleasure of a dog is that you can make a fool out of yourself and not only will he not scold you, but he will make a fool out of himself too.—Samuel Butler

My little dog, a heartbeat at my feet.—Edith Wharton

My goal in life is to be as good a person as my dog already thinks I am.—Unknown

Dogs are not our whole lives, but they make our lives whole.—Roger Caras

The dog was created especially for children. He is the God of Frolic.—Henry Ward Beecher

A dog is the only thing on earth that loves you more than he loves himself.—Josh Billings

Whoever said you couldn't buy happiness forgot all about little puppies.—Gene Hill

A dog wags its tail with its heart.—Martin Buxbaum

He is your friend, your partner, your defender, your dog. You are his life, his love, his leader. He will be yours, faithful and true, to the last beat of his heart. You owe it to him to be worthy of such devotion.—Unknown

## Cats

There are no ordinary cats.—Sidonie Gabrielle Colette

The smallest feline is a masterpiece.—Leonardo Da Vinci

To err is human, to purr is feline.—Robert Byrne

In ancient times, cats were worshipped as gods; they have not forgotten this.—Unknown

Way down deep we all have the same urges. Cats have the courage to live by them.—Jim Davis

Cats are the connoisseurs of comfort.—James Herriot

Cats seem to go on the principle that it never does any harm to ask for what you want.—Joseph Wood

If cats could talk, they wouldn't.—Nan Porter

As every cat owner knows, nobody owns a cat.—Ellen Perry

God made the cat in order that he might have the pleasure of caressing the tiger.—Fernand Mery

Dogs come when they are called; cats take a message and get back to you later.—Mary Bly

Dogs have owners, cats have staff.—Unknown

A cat is a puzzle for which there is no solution.—Hazel Nicholson

## General Animals

Ask of the beasts and they will teach you the beauty of this earth.—St. Francis of Assisi

You become responsible for that which you have tamed.—Antoine de Saint Exupery

Some of God's greatest gifts are the animals he gives us to love.—Unknown

Animals are such agreeable friends–they ask no questions, they pass no criticisms.—George Eliot

Until one has loved an animal, a part of one's soul remains unawakened.—Anatole France

## Pet Fact and Quote Resources

- http://allaboutfrogs.org
- http://www.abc.net.au/creaturefeatures/facts/default/htm
- http://www.deltasociety.org/dsc020.htm
- http://www.fernbank.edu/museum/frogs/funfrogfacts.html
- http://www.fishedz.com/funfacts.htm
- http://members.tripod.com/ndrc/dogfacts.htm
- http://www.suite101.com/article.cfm/science_for_kids/107579
- http://www.takingthelead.co.uk/2/Fun/dogfacts.htm
- http://www.xmission.com/~emailbox/trivia.htm
- www.absoluteastronomy.com
- www.doctordog.com
- www.exotictropicals.com
- www.i-pets.com
- www.Pbskids.org
- www.petsinpastel.com
- www.peturns.com
- www.rabbit.org
- www.simplypets.com

## P.1
### Best Kind of Friend (Furry)

Furry friends are some of the best kind to have, as Michele conveys with the unspoken bond illustrated in this chummy photo. Michele cut descriptive words from pet-themed patterned paper and then included a band of paper along the bottom. She placed the words along the cardstock strips to pull the eye across the page both vertically and horizontally. Michele mounted the black-and-white photo of these forever friends onto red cardstock for eye-catching contrast.

Michele Woods,
Reynoldsburg, Ohio
**Supplies:** Patterned paper (Karen Foster Design); stamping ink; pen

## P. 6
### Fletch

Here several pet-themed prints combine along with coordinating accents for a purely-dog-inspired design. Emily sectioned off her page space and covered the paper seams with printed twill for a neat and clean look. Rub-on letters were used for the title treatment, which were then cut out for dimension. Handwritten journaling commemorating Emily's love and appreciation for her canine is accented with a dog bone shaped paper clip for a subtle touch.

Emily Curry Hitchingham,
Memory Makers Books
**Supplies:** Patterned papers, printed twill, dog bone paper clip (Carolee's Creations); rub-on letters (Making Memories); pen

## P. 8
### And They Call It Puppy Love

This tender layout commemorates the day Sonny, a homeless 10-week-old golden retriever puppy, was brought to Lisa's home as a "foster dog." After his stressful day at the rescue center, Sonny plopped onto Lisa's couch where she took these adorable photographs, and he hasn't left since! Lisa used warm, rich tones, heart shapes and flower accents to convey loving emotion on this cherished puppy's page. Her simple journaling is printed inside the scored paper booklet on the upper left, accentuated by charming vintage buttons and fuzzy fibers.

Lisa M. Pace, Frisco, Texas
**Supplies:** Patterned paper (Bazzill, Daisy D's); textured cardstock (Basic Grey, DieCuts with a View); monogram letters, medium circle brads (Making Memories); chipboard coaster (Li'l Davis Designs); fibers (EK Success); rub-on letters (Jo-Ann Stores); chalk ink (Clearsnap); solvent ink (Tsukineko); yarn; vintage buttons; corner punch; T-pin; foam adhesive spacers

## P. 36
### Sun Catcher

According to Torrey's cat, Cosmo, nothing beats basking in the glow of the sun. Torrey brought the beauty and warmth of Cosmo's favorite pastime directly onto this unique layout with a yellow vellum sun and rays that radiate in and out of the page elements. For each photo, Torrey printed two copies—one in color and the other in black-and-white. Torrey cut out sections of the color photos to lie atop the identical sections of the black-and-white photos. To form the sunbeams, she added yellow vellum in between the photos and running off the page. Radiant, foam adhesive-mounted silk sunflowers complete this sunny salute to Cosmo's sunbathing.

Torrey Scott, Thornton, Colorado
**Supplies:** Patterned papers (Li'l Davis Designs, Scenic Route Paper Co.); chipboard letters (Li'l Davis Designs); silk flowers; vellum; cardstock; foam adhesive spacers

## P. 64
### Coki The Water Dragon

This Chinese water dragon has been the most gentle and funny pet Stacey's family has ever owned, so she created this dynamic design to express Coki's laid-back attitude. Deep dark background colors convey a masculine look and allow the vibrant hues of the green paper and Coki's skin to practically leap off the page. To create her camouflaged journaling block, Stacey created a text box on her computer, formatting the background to black and the font color to white.

Stacey Stamitoles, Sylvania, Ohio
**Supplies:** Patterned papers (Junkitz, Scenic Route Paper Co.); rub-on letters (Junkitz, Making Memories); monogram coaster (SEI); ribbon buckle, epoxy letters (Junkitz); rickrack (Michaels); rub-on stitching (Autumn Leaves); ribbon (May Arts); chipboard letters (Making Memories)

## P. 92
### Pals

Nothing says love quite like a "wet wipe" smooch from a sweet puppy, as revealed on Michele's heartwarming design. Michele took this photo in her garage, keeping the subjects off-center in order to have room for the words on the right. She printed the photo in sepia and layered her printed transparency over the top, highlighting the bottom phrase in blue for emphasis. The neat, crisp and well-balanced design is given a playful feel by simply setting the large photo at a slight angle, creating the look of being tackled with puppy kisses.

Michele Anderson,
Superior, Wisconsin
**Supplies:** Patterned paper (Scrapworks); textured cardstock (Bazzill); ribbons (Offray, Stampin' Up!); letter stickers (American Crafts); eyelets, metal-rimmed tag (Making Memories); transparency

# Sources

The following companies manufacture products featured in this book. Please check your local retailers to find these materials, or go to a company's Web site for the latest product. In addition, we have made every attempt to properly credit the items mentioned in this book. We apologize to any company that we have listed incorrectly, and we would appreciate hearing from you.

Our cover puppy appears courtesy of
Pamela L. Hoffman
Flyway Goldens
Platteville, Colorado

2DYE4
www.canscrapink.com

7 Gypsies
(800) 588-6707
www.7gypsies.com

Adobe Systems Incorporated
(866) 766-2256
www.adobe.com

All Night Media (see Plaid Enterprises)

Altered Paper Press- no contact info

American Art Clay Co. (AMACO)
(800) 374-1600
www.amaco.com

American Crafts
(801) 226-0747
www.americancrafts.com

American Tag Company
(800) 223-3956
www.americantag.net

American Traditional Designs®
(800) 448-6656
www.americantraditional.com

Arctic Frog
(479) 636-FROG
www.arcticfrog.com

Around The Block
(801) 593-1946
www.aroundtheblockproducts.com

Artistic Expressions
(219) 764-5158
www.artisticexpressionsinc.com

Autumn Leaves
(800) 588-6707
www.autumnleaves.com

Avery Dennison Corporation
(800) GO-AVERY
www.avery.com

Basic Grey™
(801) 451-6006
www.basicgrey.com

Bazzill Basics Paper
(480) 558-8557
www.bazzillbasics.com

Bead Heaven- no contact info

Berwick Offray, LLC
(800) 344-5533
www.offray.com

Bo-Bunny Press
(801) 771-4010
www.bobunny.com

Boxer Scrapbook Productions
(503) 625-0455
www.boxerscrapbooks.com

Buttons Galore
(856) 753-0165
www.buttonsgaloreandmore.com

Canson®, Inc.
(800) 628-9283
www.canson-us.com

Card Connection- see Michaels

Carolee's Creations®
(435) 563-1100
www.ccpaper.com

Catslife Press
(541) 902-7855
www.harborside.com

ChartPak
(800) 628-1910
www.chartpak.com

Chatterbox, Inc.
(208) 939-9133
www.chatterboxinc.com

Clearsnap, Inc.
(360) 293-6634
www.clearsnap.com

Club Scrap™, Inc.
(888) 634-9100
www.clubscrap.com

Colorbök™, Inc.
(800) 366-4660
www.colorbok.com

Color Textiles- no contact info

CottageArts.net™
www.cottagearts.net

Crayola®
www.crayola.com

Creative Expressions- no contact info

Creative Imaginations
(800) 942-6487
www.cigift.com

Creative Impressions Rubber Stamps, Inc.
(719) 596-4860
www.creativeimpressions.com

Creative Memories®
(800) 468-9335
www.creativememories.com

Creek Bank Creations, Inc.
(217) 427-5980
www.creekbankcreations.com

C.R. Gibson®
(800) 243-6004
www.crgibson.com

Daisy D's Paper Company
(888) 601-8955
www.daisydspaper.com

Déjà Views®
(800) 243-8419
www.dejaviews.com

Design Originals
(800) 877-0067
www.d-originals.com

Diane's Daughters®
(801) 621-8392
www.dianesdaughters.com

DieCuts with a View™
(877) 221-6107
www.dcwv.com

Disney Company
www.disney.com

DMC Corp.
(973) 589-0606
www.dmc.com

Doodlebug Design™ Inc.
(801) 966-9952
www.doodlebug.ws

Dymo
(800) 426-7827
www.dymo.com

Eastman Kodak Company
(770) 522-2542
www.kodak.com

EK Success™, Ltd.
(800) 524-1349
www.eksuccess.com

Emagination Crafts, Inc.
(866) 238-9770
www.emaginationcrafts.com

Fiber Accents- no contact info

Fiskars®, Inc.
(800) 950-0203
www.fiskars.com

Flair® Designs
(888) 546-9990
www.flairdesignsinc.com

FontWerks
(604) 942-3105
www.fontwerks.com

FoofaLa
(402) 330-3208
www.foofala.com

Grafix®
(800) 447-2349
www.grafix.com

Great Balls of Fiber
(303) 697-5942
www.greatballsoffiber.com

Happy Hammer, The
(303) 690-3883
www.thehappyhammer.com

Heidi Grace Designs
(866) 89heidi
www.heidigrace.com

Heidi Swapp/Advantus Corporation
(904) 482-0092
www.heidiswapp.com

Hero Arts® Rubber Stamps, Inc.
(800) 822-4376
www.heroarts.com

Hillcreek Designs
(619) 562-5799
www.hillcreekdesigns.com

Hirschberg Schutz & Co., Inc.
(800) 221-8640

Hobby Lobby Stores, Inc.
www.hobbylobby.com

Home Depot U.S.A., Inc.
www.homedepot.com

Hot Off The Press, Inc.
(800) 227-9595
www.paperpizazz.com

Imagination Project, Inc.
(513) 860-2711
www.imaginationproject.com

jcaroline creative!
www.jcarolinecreative.com

Jesse James & Co., Inc.
(610) 435-0201
www.jessejamesbutton.com

Jest Charming
(702) 564-5101
www.jestcharming.com

JHB International
(303) 751-8100
www.buttons.com

Jo-Ann Stores
(888) 739-4120
www.joann.com

JudiKins
(310) 515-1115
www.judikins.com

June Tailor
(800) 844-5400
www.junetailor.com

Junkitz™
(732) 792-1108
www.junkitz.com

K & Company
(888) 244-2083
www.kandcompany.com

Karen Foster Design
(801) 451-9779
www.karenfosterdesign.com

Keepsake Designs
www.keepsakedesigns.biz

KI Memories
(972) 243-5595
www.kimemories.com

Kopp Design
(801) 489-6011
www.koppdesign.com

Lasting Impressions for Paper, Inc.
(801) 298-1979
www.lastingimpressions.com

Leave Memories
www.leavememories.com

Legacy Paper Arts- no contact info

Li'l Davis Designs
(949) 838-0344
www.lildavisdesigns.com

Limited Edition Rubberstamps
(650) 594-4242
www.limitededitionrs.com

M & J Trimming
(800) 9-MJTRIM
www.mjtrim.com

Magenta Rubber Stamps
(800) 565-5254
www.magentastyle.com

Magic Mesh
(651) 345-6374
www.magicmesh.com

Magic Scraps™
(972) 238-1838
www.magicscraps.com

Magnetic Poetry®
(800) 370-7697
www.magneticpoetry.com

Making Memories
(800) 286-5263
www.makingmemories.com

Mara-Mi, Inc.
(800) 627-2648
www.mara-mi.com

Marvy® Uchida/Uchida of America, Corp.
(800) 541-5877
www.uchida.com

Ma Vinci's Reliquary
http://crafts.dm.net/mall/reliquary/

Maya Road, LLC
(214) 488-3279
www.mayaroad.com

May Arts
(800) 442-3950
www.mayarts.com

me & my BiG ideas®
(949) 883-2065
www.meandmybigideas.com

Melissa Frances/Heart & Home, Inc.
(905) 686-9031
www.melissafrances.com

Memories Complete™, LLC
(866) 966-6365
www.memoriescomplete.com

Michaels® Arts & Crafts
(800) 642-4235
www.michaels.com

Microsoft Corporation
www.microsoft.com

MoBe' Stamps!
(925) 443-2101
www.mobestamps.com

MOD-my own design
(303) 641-8680
www.mod-myowndesign.com

Morex Corporation
(717) 852-7771
www.morexcorp.com

Mustard Moon™
(408) 299-8542
www.mustardmoon.com

My Mind's Eye™, Inc.
(800) 665-5116
www.frame-ups.com

Nunn Design
(360) 379-3557
www.nunndesign.com

Office Max
www.officemax.com

Offray- see Berwick Offray, LLC

Outdoors & More Scrapbook Decor
(801) 390-6919
www.outdoorsandmore.com

Paperbilities- no contact info

Paper Fever, Inc.
(800) 477-0902
www.paperfever.com

Paper House Productions®
(800) 255-7316
www.paperhouseproductions.com

Paper Loft
(866) 254-1961
www.paperloft.com

Paper Reflections- no contact info

Pebbles Inc.
(801) 224-1857
www.pebblesinc.com

Pinecone Press
(714) 434-9881
www.pineconepressbooks.com

Plaid Enterprises, Inc.
(800) 842-4197
www.plaidonline.com

Postmodern Design
(405) 321-3176
www.stampdiva.com

Prima Marketing, Inc.
(909) 627-5532
www.mulberrypaperflowers.com

Primitive Barn- no contact info

Provo Craft®
(888) 577-3545
www.provocraft.com

PSX Design™
(800) 782-6748
www.psxdesign.com

Punch Bunch, The
(254) 791-4209
www.thepunchbunch.com

Purple Onion Designs
www.purpleoniondesigns.com

Queen & Co.
(858) 485-5132
www.queenandcompany.com

QuicKutz, Inc.
(801) 765-1144
www.quickutz.com

Ranger Industries, Inc.
(800) 244-2211
www.rangerink.com

River City Rubber Works
(877) 735-2276
www.rivercityrubberworks.com

Rusty Pickle
(801) 746-1045
www.rustypickle.com

Sakura Hobby Craft
(310) 212-7878
www.sakuracraft.com

Sarah Heidt Photo Craft, LLC
(734) 424-2776
www.sarahheidtphotocraft.com

Scenic Route Paper Co.
(801) 785-0761
www.scenicroutepaper.com

Scrapbooking Society, The
(914) 474-5447
www.scrapbooksociety.com

Scrapbook Trends Magazine
(888) 225-9199
www.scrapbooktrendsmag.com

Scraps and Scribbles- no contact info

Scraptivity™ Scrapbooking, Inc.
(800) 393-2151
www.scraptivity.com

Scrapworks, LLC
(801) 363-1010
www.scrapworks.com

SEI, Inc.
(800) 333-3279
www.shopsei.com

Sizzix
(866) 742-4447
www.sizzix.com

Stampabilities®
(800) 888-0321
www.stampabilities.com

Stamp Cabana- no contact info

Stamp Craft- see Plaid Enterprises

Stampendous!®
(800) 869-0474
www.stampendous.com

Stamping Sensations
(815) 589-4100
www.stampingsensations.com

Stampington & Company
(877) STAMPER
www.stampington.com

Stampin' Up!®
(800) 782-6787
www.stampinup.com

Stamps Happen, Inc.®
(714) 879-9894
www.stampshappen.com

Sticker Studio™
(208) 322-2465
www.stickerstudio.com

Sweetwater
(800) 359-3094
www.sweetwaterscrapbook.com

Target
www.target.com

Technique Tuesday, LLC
(503) 644-4073
www.techniquetuesday.com

Therm O Web, Inc.
(800) 323-0799
www.thermoweb.com

Top Line Creations™
(866) 954-0559
www.topline-creations.com

Treehouse Designs
(501) 372-1109
www.treehouse-designs.com

Tsukineko®, Inc.
(800) 769-6633
www.tsukineko.com

Urban Lily- no contact info

Wal-Mart Stores, Inc.
(800) WALMART
www.walmart.com

Warmcuddles Embellishments
www.warmcuddles.com

Westrim® Crafts
(800) 727-2727
www.westrimcrafts.com

Whispers- no contact info

Wintech International Corp.
(800) 263-6043
www.wintechint.com

Wishblade™, Inc.
(651) 644-5144
www.wishblade.com

Wordsworth
(719) 282-3495
www.wordsworthstamps.com

WorldWin Paper
(888) 843-6455
www.thepapermill.com

Wrights® Ribbon Accents
(877) 597-4448
www.wrights.com

Xyron
(800) 793-3523
www.xyron.com

Yvonne Albrighton- no contact info

# Index

## Look for these other outstanding Memory Makers Books

*All Men Scrapbook Pages*
ISBN-13: 978-1-892127-67-9
ISBN-10: 1-892127-67-9
paperback, 112 pgs., #33441

*All Kids Scrapbook Pages*
ISBN-13: 978-1-892127-63-1
ISBN-10: 1-892127-63-6
paperback, 112 pgs., #33440

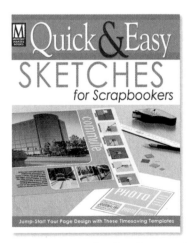

*Quick & Easy Sketches for Scrapbookers*
ISBN-13: 978-1-892127-64-8
ISBN-10: 1-892127-64-4
paperback, 96 pgs., #33436

These books and other fine Memory Makers Books titles are available from your local art or craft retailer, bookstore or online supplier. Please see page 2 of this book for contact information for Canada, Australia, the U.K. and Europe.